A JUDE 3 PROJECT CURRICULUM

THROUGH EYES OF COLOR

A CONTEXTUALIZED GUIDE TO HELP YOU KNOW WHAT YOU BELIEVE AND WHY.

CURATED BY: LISA FIELDS

WRITTEN BY: YANA CONNER

Jude 3 Project, Inc.
PO Box 26206
Jacksonville, FL 32226

www.jude3project.org

Contents

Introduction

"I'm going to change everything you thought about Jesus." Those were the first words that signaled that my New Testament course at the University of North Florida was not going to be like Sunday school. I grew up in church and knew the Bible, so I didn't expect this class to be a challenge, but it was. Thankfully, my father connected the dots for me by introducing me to an apologetic ministry called Ravi Zacharias International Ministries. Apologetics was a foreign concept to me as it probably is to many of you who are starting this curriculum. You may be thinking, "are we about to apologize for our belief in God?" I get it. In the Bible, Peter instructs believers in 1 Peter 3:15 to be able to give a "defense" for the hope they have. That word "defense" is a translation for the Greek word "apologia". This is where we get the word apologetics. Apologetics is simply explaining why you believe what you believe with gentleness and respect.

This strikes at the core of the mission and vision of the Jude 3 Project, which is to help black Christians know what they believe and why they believe it. You cannot defend a faith you cannot define. Before you can go into the world and give a defense for your faith, you need to think critically about what you believe and why. I did not realize the importance of this until I was challenged in college. Being challenged was not the end of my faith, it was the beginning of it being strengthened. As my Old Testament professor used to tell us, "God is big enough for our questions." I've come to believe that God is not only big enough for our questions, but He gives us the freedom to ask them.

One of the initial ways we have been able to help black Christians become equipped in defending their faith is through our podcast. We were excited to learn that pastors across the country were using our podcast in their Bible studies and small groups. To further equip them, we decided to create a curriculum around some of our more popular episodes and provide a more structured way to engage in relevant topics for black Christians.

As you begin this curriculum, you or your group, will embark on a six-week journey into apologetics through the eyes of color. The first chapter will help you with Bible study basics. The Bible is our guide and it's important that we know how to handle it correctly. The second chapter will explore black figures in the Bible. This helps us as black people to see ourselves in the faith that we hold near and dear to our identity. The third chapter will explore early African Christianity. The connection between black people and Christianity did not start in the era of slavery and it's important that we know our history to engage those who think it does. The next chapter will be focusing on black Christians in America and their contributions to the black church. Chapter five will provide some helpful tools to address black cults like the Nation of Islam and Hebrew Israelites. The final chapter will address several places of contention within the Bible that are hard to understand and may raise eyebrows. We want to give you some helpful tools to address some of those challenging passages, including those concerning women and slavery.

We pray that your faith will be strengthened once you have completed this curriculum and you will be better equipped to contend for the faith, not for argument's sake but for the sake of transformational and courageous conversations. Remember, apologetics is not about winning arguments but winning people. Apologetics is not just about an intellectual exercise, it's also incarnational. What good is it to give intellectual reasons for why skeptics should trust the Bible if you don't live under its authority? In addition to equipping yourself with this curriculum, we challenge you to embody the message. Giving a defense falls on deaf ears if our lives don't back it up.

We hope you enjoy this six week journey through the eyes of color!

Grace & Peace,

Lisa Fields
Founder & President
Jude 3 Project

Leader's Guide

CHAPTER ONE

Objective

To provide participants with a foundation for how to study the Bible.

Big Ideas

1. In order to effectively "contend for the faith," you must know it. You can't defend what you don't know. But before we can discuss how to provide an apology for Christianity, we need to equip you with tools for studying the Bible you seek to defend.
2. We do not engage in hermeneutics for the sole purpose of contending for the faith. We practice hermeneutics to know and worship God by bringing our lives into harmony with His character and will. If you picked up this resource in hopes that you would be able to argue down that radical sister who intellectually laid you out, can we offer you a greater goal? Don't do apologetics merely for others. Do apologetics for your own sake. Do apologetics to ensure you see God for who He truly is amid religions and ideologies that would seek to distort or erase Him.

JUDE 3 PROJECT

Podcast Playlist

"The Importance of Biblical Literacy"
Guest: Dr. Cynthia James
Date: October 2017

"Interpreting Scripture 101"
Guest: Dr. Luke Brad Bobo
Date: September 2018

Helpful Tips

Tip 1: Since this is your first time meeting, have each participant share what they hope to gain from this study. Share with your group your expectations regarding homework. Set ground rules for communicating to ensure you are creating a safe space for people to share their concerns and ask their seemingly dumb questions. Be sure to also spend some time in prayer about your desired outcomes.

Tip 2: During this study, you and your group will spend some time studying God's Word together. If you can, have a study Bible and commentaries on hand for your group to interact with during your study of 2 Peter. You can ask your pastor for one or check one out from the library. Consult bestcommentaries.com for the good ones though—there are some bad commentaries out there. If you can't find a commentary (and even if you can), consider using an online Bible study tool such as blueletterbible.com to give your group an opportunity to dig deeper. This way they can learn how to use these resources on their own. Blue Letter Bible is an excellent resource to consult for defining key terms. Be sure to practice on your own with these tools before presenting them to the group.

Chapter One

WHAT IS HERMENEUTICS?

I. What is Hermeneutics?

In order to effectively "contend for the faith", you must know it. In this chapter, we are going to build a foundation for how to study the Bible. Scholars refer to this laborious yet fruitful process as hermeneutics. Hermeneutics is the art and science of biblical interpretation. It is an art because, like skilled artists, we must know which "brush" to use to enhance our understanding of a biblical passage. It is a science because, like scientists, we must follow a careful method of observation, interpretation, and application.

However, we do not engage in hermeneutics for the sole purpose of contending for the faith. We practice hermeneutics to know and worship God by bringing our lives into harmony with His character and will. Once the word of God has a hold of us, we are in a better position to interact with the world around us.

KNOW GOD

In his Jude 3 Project podcast interview, Interpreting Scripture 101, Dr. Luke Bobo said, "One of the ways we know our God deeply is through Bible study."[1] Though creation gives us a sense of God's existence and power, it's only through the Bible that

1. Bobo, Luke Brad. The Jude 3 Project. (2018, September). Interpreting Scripture 101. [Audio podcast]. Retrieved from URL.

we encounter the "nothing-is-too-hard-for-Him" God of Abraham—the "I AM" who delivered Israel and resurrected the Savior, Jesus Christ, who came to take away the sins of the world. Without these historical accounts, we would have little to no knowledge of God's holy character or His love for the world. God's Word (the Bible) is a gift to us.

WORSHIP GOD

Knowledge of God isn't just information about God that takes up space in our minds. It's supposed to do something (2 Peter 1:5–11). As we become more acquainted with the God of the Bible, He radically changes our lives. We move from being enemies of God to worshippers of Him. Our thoughts, affections, and actions are all made new.

If our knowledge of God only results in us gaining the ability to effectively "contend for the faith" and doesn't change our lives, we have completely missed the point.

What is the best gift you've ever given a person? Why did you give them that particular gift?

How would it make you feel if they used that gift in a way that you didn't intend for them to use it?

How would you feel if that gift was left unopened?

II. Unwrapping the Gift

In this section, we are going to learn how to properly unwrap the gift of God's Word for the sake of knowing and worshipping Him by using five intentional steps.

STEP 1: GET STILL

When you open the Bible, you come face to face with God. It is important to open God's Word with a posture of reverence and expectation. Opening your Bible with reverence means doing so with a heart full of thankfulness for the gift of being able to encounter the living God through His Word. Then, expect the eyes of your heart to be enlightened so that you may know with a greater sense of clarity and assurance the hope to which you've been called in Jesus Christ (Ephesians 1:18).

- Get in a place where you can meet with the Lord undistracted.
- Settle your heart through prayer.
- Ask the Holy Spirit, who has been given to you and lives inside you, to lead you into all truth.

STEP 2: GET FAMILIAR

The best way to get familiar with a passage you are studying is to read it repeatedly over and over again. As you read, pay attention to repeated words and phrases. This helps you see the main point the author is seeking to get across to his readers. Also, take note of conjunctions such as, "but," "therefore," or others like these. These words usually signify important transitions to help us understand the flow of the passage. Consider the "but" in Matthew 5:21-22:

"You have heard that our ancestors were told, 'You must not murder.
If you commit murder, you are subject to judgement.'
But I say, if you are even angry with someone, you are subject to judgement!"

What role does "but" play in this passage?

What are the similar and contrasting elements surrounding "but"?

How does comparing and contrasting these elements deepen your understanding of Jesus's command?

STEP 3: GET CURIOUS

LifeWay Research reports that although most Americans have a positive view of the Bible, only eleven percent of them have actually read it cover to cover. LifeWay also reports that, regarding our intake of the Bible, thirty-five percent of Americans only pick up the Bible when they need to, nineteen percent stick to only re-reading their favorite parts, and seventeen percent just shake the Bible like an eight-ball and read a passage at random. Then there are the thirty percent who have never read it.

Dr. Cynthia James offers two responses to the question "Why do you think that a lot people who own Bibles don't read them?":

- There are some who have come to view the Bible as a "dead document" that doesn't have any relevance for their lives.
- To really engage the Bible as a treasure and hold it dear, you have to work.[2]

Though Dr. James admits this is not an exhaustive list of reasons to explain why people don't read their Bible, it's clear that many have lost either their interest or curiosity in the Bible. But when we get curious and do the hard work of asking the passage questions, the Bible comes alive. Scholars refer to this process as "interrogating the

---

2. James, Cynthia. The Jude 3 Project. (2017, October). The Importance of Biblical Literacy. [Audio podcast]. Retrieved from URL.

text." Here are some helpful interrogation questions to get you started:

Who wrote this passage?

This information is usually found at the beginning of the book you are studying. If not, the title of the book often identifies the author.

Who was the passage written for?

This information is usually found at the beginning of the book you are studying. When studying the Old Testament or a New Testament book where a recipient is not identified, consider it as a book that was written for future generations of Israelites.

Why was this written?

This is an important question to ask because you want to understand the author's intent in writing the book. (i.e., Why did Paul write letters to the church at Corinth? Why did Moses write down all those laws in Leviticus?)

What does this mean?

If there is ever a word, phrase, or statement you don't understand, ask the question, "What does it mean?" Don't just brush over it. Make note of it with the intention to find the answer.

STEP 4: GET UNDERSTANDING

Opening the Bible is like stepping into a foreign country. We encounter unfamiliar language and customs, stories that don't make sense through our twenty-first century colored eyes, and passages that cause us to question our understanding of God. It can feel a lot like being on the outside of an inside joke. And let's be real, this is probably the biggest barrier to reading the Bible.

But here's the good news: God has provided us with everything we need to correctly interpret and understand His Word! He has given us:

His Spirit

The One who is an insider on all the works of the triune God lives inside of you (John 16:12–15). FACTS!

His Word

Many of the answers to our questions about a passage can be found in the Bible. If you are trying to understand circumcision in the New Testament, for instance, you can find some clarity in the Old Testament. If you read Jeremiah 29:11 and want to know who Jeremiah was writing to and why he was writing to them, you only need to read verses 1–10. Scholars refer to this as the "literary context," and it is essential to the science of biblical interpretation.

His People

If you find yourself stumped and unable to find the answer to your questions, go ask someone in your church or your family who you trust. Don't let pride or fear keep you from growing.

For centuries, brothers and sisters of the faith have studied the Word and written down their findings to help the Church better understand God's Word. This is a tremendous blessing to us because there will be times when you need to pick up a study Bible or commentary to find answers to your questions. This usually happens when we have questions about the historical and cultural context of the passage.

What keeps you from reading the Bible?

STEP 5: GET REAL

As stated before, we study God's Word for the sake of knowing and worshipping Him by bringing our whole life into harmony with His character and will. Now that you have done the hard work of unwrapping the knowledge of God's Word, it's time to apply that knowledge to your life. Here are some questions to ask yourself:

- How would I summarize this passage in my own words?
- Is there a truth I need to accept and believe?
- Is there a sin I need to confess?
- Is there a person I need to ask for forgiveness or accountability?

- Is there a behavior I need to adopt?
- What do I need to ask the Lord to help me with in light of this passage?

III. Unwrapping 2 Peter 1:5–9

"In view of all this, make every effort to respond to God's promises. Supplement your faith with a generous provision of moral excellence, and moral excellence with knowledge, and knowledge with self-control, and self-control with patient endurance, and patient endurance with godliness, and godliness with brotherly affection, and brotherly affection with love for everyone. The more you grow like this the more productive and useful you will be in your knowledge of our Lord Jesus Christ. But those who fail to develop in this way are shortsighted or blind, forgetting that they have been cleansed from their old sins."

2 Peter 1:5–9

STEP 1: GET STILL

Pray as a group that God would speak to you through His Word.

STEP 2: GET FAMILIAR

Read through the passage as a group three times.

- The first time have someone read the passage aloud slowly.
- The second time have each person read it to themselves.
- The third time have someone read aloud slowly, but this time look for repeated words, phrases, and conjunctions.

What words and phrases are repeated in this passage?

What is the author emphasizing by repeatedly using these words or phrases?

What are the conjunctions in this passage?

What role does each conjunction play in the passage? How is it being used?

STEP 3: GET CURIOUS

Who wrote this passage?

Who is the passage written for?

What is the phrase "In view of all this" pointing back to? How does this deepen your understanding of the passage?

What are some key terms you need to define?

What other questions do you have about this passage?

STEP 4: GET UNDERSTANDING

In this section, do your best to find the answers to your questions about the passage by using the Bible and a trusted study Bible. You might also want to use a dictionary or concordance to define the key terms you listed in the previous section. Don't worry if you can't find the answers to all your questions. It's a process. Pocket those unresolved questions and seek out a trusted friend or commentary for help later.

What is the author's main point in this passage?

How would you summarize this passage in your own words?

STEP 5: GET REAL

In light of your discussion and understanding of the text, consider how God is leading you to respond:

- Is there a truth I need to accept and believe?
- Is there a sin I need to confess?
- Is there a person I need to ask for forgiveness or accountability?
- Is there a behavior I need to adopt?
- What do I need to ask the Lord to help me with in light of this passage?

IV. TOOLS FOR GOING DEEPER

- New Living Translation: Life Application Bible
- Christian Standard Bible: Study Bible
- Bobo, Luke Brad. A Layperson's Guide to Biblical Interpretation: A Means to Know the Personal God. Eugene, Oregon: Resource Publications, 2016.
- Plummer, Robert L. 40 Questions About Interpreting the Bible. Grand Rapids, MI: Kregel Publications, 2006.

Leader's Guide

CHAPTER TWO

Objective

To expose participants to many of the black people whose stories exist in the Bible.

Big Ideas

1. Christianity is not a white man's religion. The very fact that black people are present in the Bible dismantles the idea that Christianity is a white man's religion.
2. Black history doesn't start with shackles, slave ships, and unjust labor. Black history finds its origins on the first pages of the Bible. Please don't let the narrative of American history be the primary source of shaping your black identity. Let the Word of God be your foundation, because the God of the Bible created, affirms, and delights in your blackness.
3. We don't contend for the presence of black people in the Bible because of what it says about us, but because of what is says about God. Black apologetics is not about us. It's not about proving the significance of our existence. It's about proclaiming the existence of God as He truly is. His promise to Abraham, along with His pursuit of the Ethiopian eunuch, testify that He is an inclusive and impartial Savior.

JUDE 3 PROJECT

Podcast Playlist

"Is Christianity a White Man's Religion?"
Guests: Dr. Eric Mason and Dr. Howard-John Wesley
Date: March 2017

"Black People in the Bible"
Guest: Marcus Jenkins
Date: March 2019

Helpful Tips

Tip 1: Since the group has read the material ahead of time and worked through the questions, select the paragraphs and sections you would like to read together before working through their respective questions. This way you can review and discuss the content you found important and impactful before working through the questions. However, don't get preachy. Remember, your role as the leader is to facilitate a dialogue, not gather a group of people for a monologue.

Tip 2: Be sure to emphasize the three points made under the "Why does this matter?" section. This section safeguards us from assuming an ideal of black supremacy, which shapes black cults like the Nation of Islam and Hebrew Israelites and causes them to deem other nationalities as spiritually inferior. As a group, fight against the temptation to use this information solely as a defense for your self-worth. This is about God and His glory being displaying in all the earth (Colossians 1:15–18).

Chapter Two

BLACK PEOPLE IN THE BIBLE

I. Is Christianity a White Man's Religion?

There's a lot of debate today around the question: "Is Christianity a white man's religion?" But this is not a new question.

In his Jude 3 Project interview, Dr. Eric Mason explains that this question finds its beginnings in the teachings of the Honorable Elijah Muhammad, who led the Nation of Islam from 1934 until his death in 1975.[3] In his book *Message to the Blackman in America*, Muhammad calls for African-Americans to "throw off the shackles of Christianity."[4] He writes, "There is no hope for us in Christianity; it is a religion organized by the enemies (the white race) of the Black Nation to enslave us to the white race's rule."[5]

---

3. Eric Mason and Howard-John Wesley, "Is Christianity a White Man's Religion?" [Audio podcast]. Retrieved from https://itunes.apple.com/us/podcast/courageous-conversations-v-is-christianity-white-mans/id978012810?i=1000383272786&mt=2. The Jude 3 Project (March 2017).

4. Elijah Muhammad, Message to the Blackman in America (Irving, TX: Secretarius MEMPS Publication, 1965 and 1975) 13.

5. Ibid., 161.

Though Muhammad's conclusion is inaccurate, it's easy to understand how he got there. Muhammad was a black man who was only one generation removed from slavery and a leader of a religious and political movement during the Civil Rights era. He sincerely longed for his people to be free from every source of oppression. And unfortunately, at that time and decades prior, Christianity and the Bible was used by white men and women to justify their abuse of black people. The Bible was even used as a tool to "whip" black slaves into submission when they opposed their white masters.

This is incredibly sad and evil.

Muhammad's conclusion about Christianity and the Bible was a genuine response to white men and women's heretical interpretation and application of God's Word. The consequences of their misinterpretations serve as a reminder to be diligent in our study of the scriptures.

On one of the first days of His ministry, Jesus stood up in a Jewish synagogue and proclaimed that one of the distinguishing marks of His coming kingdom would be the setting free of the oppressed (Luke 4:17–21). It must've saddened His heart greatly to hear Muhammad say, "There is no hope for black people in Christianity," when He had come to bring hope and freedom to every person of every color.

Why do you think this question—Is Christianity a white man's religion?—has recently resurfaced among people of African descent?

How would you respond if asked, "Is Christianity a white man's religion?"

II. How Do We Contend Against the Lie?

There are several ways Christians can contend against the lie that Christianity is a "white man's religion." We can point out that Jesus was a Jewish man who likely had brown eyes, olive to brown skin, and short brown curly hair.[6] There was nothing white about Him. Plus, it doesn't make much sense for a Jewish man to only provide salvation for white people.

We could also challenge the claim by drawing attention to God's promise to Abraham that "all the peoples on earth will be blessed" through him (Genesis 12:3 CSB). That's all peoples. Red, yellow, black, and white. They are all equally precious and will all equally be blessed through faith in Jesus Christ.

Read Romans 4.

What made Abraham right with God?

What makes a Jew right with God?

What makes a Gentile (a non-Jewish person) right with God?

6. Sarah Pruitt, The Ongoing Mystery of Jesus's Face. Retrieved March 27, 2019 from https://www.history.com/news/what-did-jesus-look-like.

In Romans 4, the Apostle Paul makes it clear that Christianity is neither a Jewish nor a Gentile religion. If this is true—and it is—there's no way that Christianity is a white man's religion!

Christianity is the proclamation that Jesus Christ has come into this world to save sinners and that all who would put their faith in Christ will be made right with God (Romans 3:23–26). As Rev. Walter Arthur McCray says in his book *The Black Presence in the Bible*, "For all people from every race and ethnic group ... have sinned and have fallen short of God's glory ... [and] it is revealed in the Bible that every group of people are included in God's redemption circle."[7]

We are one of them.

One other way we can contend against this sad idea that "there is no hope for black people in Christianity," is to uncover the presence of black people in the Bible. Because, let's just be real: A story becomes way more appealing to someone when they have something in common with its characters. This is why so many black people flocked to movie theaters in their African attire to see Black Panther and continue to make Xs over their chests. (Wakanda forever!)

How much more will those who once believed there was no hope for them in Christianity because of the color of their skin flock to God when they hear that they have been a part of His story since the very beginning?

III. Where Does Black History Begin?

Brothers and sisters, our history doesn't start with shackles, slave ships, and unjust labor. Our history finds its origins in the very first pages of the Bible.

Our history, along with that of every ethnic group in the world, begins in Genesis 10. Here we find what scholars refer to as the "Table of Nations"—a genealogical record of Noah and his three sons, and the nations birthed through each of them.

---

7. Walter Arthur McCray, The Black Presence In the Bible: Discovering The Black and African Identity of Biblical Persons and Nations (Chicago, IL: Black Light Fellowship, 1990) 30.

Read Genesis 10.

Genesis 10 may just seem like a list of names that are hard to pronounce, but this is the world's family tree. Those of Jewish and Arab descent trace their origins to the sons of Shem.[8] Those of European descent find their beginning in the sons of Japheth. And those of African, Asian, and Indian descent find theirs in the sons of Ham.[9]

Now, it may feel like a massive bomb has just been dropped, but there's a great wealth of biblical, historical, cultural, anthropological, geographical, and linguistic (language) evidence to support these statements. If you would like to study this topic further (which by the way is strongly encouraged), please take a look at any of the resources cited in the endnotes or listed in the "Tools for Going Deeper" section. For this introductory study, we will only explore some of the evidence that has been uncovered.

IT'S ALL IN THE NAME

In the biblical world, names carried a great deal of meaning and were often used to describe a person or group. In the original Hebrew, for instance, "Ham" means "hot" or "warm."[10] Many scholars believe this to be a reference to the heat from the sun that produces darker skin.[11] Though this might seem like a stretch, the argument gets stronger when we take a closer look at the name "Cush."

In the Bible, Cush is not only the name of one of the sons of Ham. It's also the name of the place Cush descendants settled, which was south of Egypt and west of the Nile River. Over time, Cush's name was changed to Ethiopia, and its people were no longer referred to as Cushites, but Ethiopians. Why the switch?

---

8. D. N Freedman, G.A. Herion, F.D. Graf, J.D. Pleins, and A. B. Beck, The Anchor Yale Bible Dictionary (New York: Doubleday, 1992).

9. W.A. Elwell and B.J. Beitzel, "Ham (Person)," in Baker Encyclopedia of the Bible, Vol. 1 (Grand Rapids, MI: Baker Book House, 1988) 919. William Dwight McKissic, Beyond Roots: In Search of Blacks in the Bible (Wenonah, NJ: Renaissance Productions, 1990).

10. J. Swanson, J., Dictionary of Biblical Languages with Semantic Domains: Hebrew (Old Testament) (electronic ed.). (Oak Harbor: Logos Research Systems, Inc., 1997).

11. Walter Arthur McCray, The Black Presence In the Bible: Discovering The Black and African Identity of Biblical Persons and Nations (Chicago, IL: Black Light Fellowship, 1990) 20.

The Baker Encyclopedia of the Bible (BEB) explains: "The name Ethiopia was of Greek origin, and according to some interpreters meant 'burnt-faced,' as in faces that have been burnt/blackened by the sun."[12] This helps us understand why scholars have come to accept Ham's name as hinting at his blackness.

IT'S IN THE ARCHAEOLOGICAL DATA

In Biblical and Theological Issues on the Black Presence in the Bible, Dr. Charles B. Copher presents a variety of archaeological data to support the presence of black people in Egypt and Cush (Ethiopia). Regarding historical writings, Copher shares that Herodotus (c. 484 BC–c. 425), an ancient Greek historian, describes those who were living in the "colony of Egyptians" as having "black skins and frizzled hair."[13] As it relates to paintings, he mentions several paintings of Egyptians that depicted them as having reddish brown to black skin.[14]

IV. Who Are the Black People in the Bible?

Given our brief investigation of the evidence for black people in the Bible, we're now in a better position to identify some of them. Below you will find a few people that we can identify as black based on the kind of evidence we just reviewed.

Genesis

Ham (Genesis 10)
Cush (Genesis 10)
Egypt (Genesis 10)
Hagar (Genesis 16): Hagar, the slave of Abraham and Sarah, was an Egyptian woman.

Numbers

Moses' Wife (Numbers 12:1): Moses marries a Cushite woman.

Psalms

The words of the Cushite (Psalm 7)

12. W.A. Elwell and B.J. Beitzel, "Ham (Person)," in Baker Encyclopedia of the Bible, Vol. 1 (Grand Rapids, MI: Baker Book House, 1988) 727–729.

13. Charles B. Copher, Biblical and Theological Issues on the Black Presence In the Bible (Chicago, IL: Black Light Fellowship, 1993) 23.

14. Ibid., pg. 27

Manasseh and Ephraim (Genesis 41:50–52): the sons of Joseph and his Egyptian wife, Asenath.

1 Kings

Queen Sheba (1 Kings 10:1-13): Though there is some debate about where Queen Sheba is from, many scholars have come to believe she was a queen in Ethiopia and Egypt.

Songs of Songs

The Shulamite Woman (Songs of Songs 1:5–6) : The Shulamite woman, who was the object of Solomon's affection, describes herself as being as black.

Mark

Simon of Cyrene (Mark 15:21): Though there is some debate, some scholars believe Simon was black because Cyrene had a significant population of black people in it.

Zephaniah

Zephaniah 1:1: Zephaniah's is the son of a man named "Cushi."

Acts

The Ethiopian Eunuch (Acts 8:26-40)
Simeon who was called Niger (Acts 13:1): Simeon's nickname "Niger" literally means "black." Simeon was one of leaders at the church of Antioch; the church that commissioned Barnabas and Paul to preach the gospel to the Gentiles.

Lucius of Cyrene (Acts 13:1): Though there is some debate, a number of scholars believe Lucius was black because Cyrene had a significant population of black people. Lucius was one of leaders at the church of Antioch; the church that commissioned Barnabas and Paul to preach the gospel to the Gentiles.

V. Why Does This Matter?

Why does the presence of black people in the Bible matter?

Here are three additional reasons why the discussion of the presence of black people in the Bible matters:

The presence of black people in the Bible matters because the Bible is the inspired

Word of God. Everything God does is intentional. There is not one word or one story in the Bible that was included haphazardly. Instead, God intentionally inspired the writers of Scripture to record particular stories. Who they were in regard to their ethnicity, gender, and socio-economic status mattered to God. When we fail to pay attention to these things, we limit our ability to interpret and apply the meaning of these stories to our lives.

Read the story of the Ethiopian eunuch recorded in Acts 8:26–40.

Philip, who was a disciple of Christ, received a message from the Lord to get up and head south to the road that runs from Jerusalem to Gaza at a time when his ministry in Samaria was going very well. Why would God call Philip away from a successful ministry to go to a desert road to meet the Ethiopian eunuch?

Ph.D. student Marcus Jerkins explains in his Jude 3 podcast episode that as a black man and a eunuch, the Ethiopian man would have experienced a lot of humiliation.[15] *How do you think it impacted him to hear that Christ, whose appearance was also not desirable, had endured humiliation and injustice so that he could be made right with God (Isaiah 53:2)?*

The presence of black people in the Bible matters because their stories give hope to people of color who have been often stripped of their dignity and intrinsic value.

Read the story of Hagar recorded in Genesis 16.

Hagar is a passive participant in this story. She gets no say as to whether she's on board with

15. Marcus Jenkins, The Jude 3 Project. (2019, March). Black People in the Bible. [Audio podcast]. Retrieved from http://www.jude3project.com/podcast/black (March 2019).

Abram and Sarah's plan, yet she bears all the consequences of their decision. What kind of impact do you think it had for her to be visited by an angel of the Lord?

In this story, Hagar goes from not being seen by her slave owners to being seen by the living God! She is also the first person in the Bible to give a name to God: "El-Roi," which means "you are the God who sees." What does Hagar's story teach you about our God?

The presence of black people in the Bible matters because it reveals that God doesn't play favorites. We don't contend for the presence of black people in the Bible because of what it says about us, but because of what is says about God. As we see in the stories of the Ethiopian eunuch and Hagar, God wants everyone to come to a saving knowledge of Him through Jesus Christ. The idea that Christianity is a white man's religion defames God's character and distorts His plans.

Read Romans 3:21–31.

Use the five-step process for Bible study presented in the last chapter to unwrap the meaning of this passage and its implications for us.

Given what you have learned from this study, would you response to the question, "Is Christianity a white man's religion?," be different? If so, how?

VI. TOOLS FOR GOING DEEPER

- Walter Arthur McCray, The Black Presence in the Bible: Discovering the Black and African Identity of Biblical Persons and Nations (Chicago, IL: Black Light Fellowship, 1990).
- William Dwight McKissic, Beyond Roots: In Search of Blacks In the Bible (Wenonah, NJ: Renaissance Productions, 1990).
- Charles B. Copher, Biblical and Theological Issues on the Black Presence In the Bible (Chicago, IL: Black Light Fellowship, 1993).

Leader's Guide

CHAPTER THREE

Objective

To prove that Christianity has deep African roots.

Big Ideas

1. Africa played a decisive role in the formation of Christian culture. "Decisive intellectual achievements of Christianity were explored and understood first in Africa before they were recognized in Europe, and a millennium before they found their way to North America." — Dr. Thomas C. Oden, How Africa Shaped the Christian Mind
2. Many have come to reject Christianity not because they have issues with Jesus, but because they primarily associate Christianity with colonialism and slavery. This rejection is short-sighted because they haven't gone back far enough into history to see how Christianity has deep African roots.
3. Some have said if it wasn't for slavery, African Americans would've never heard and received the Gospel of Jesus Christ. This is a lie. The little bit of evidence presented in this chapter proves that long before America was discovered, Christianity had already taken root in Africa in a powerful and meaningful way.

JUDE 3 PROJECT

Podcast Playlist

"Is Christianity a White Man's Religion?"
Guest: Dr. Vince Bantu
Date: June 2016

"The Life and Word of Athanasius"
Guest: Dr. John Tyson
Date: August 2017

"The African Roots of the Reformation"
Guest: Dr. David Daniels
Date: November 2017

Helpful Tips

Tip 1: Just as last time, read the material ahead of time and select sections you would like to read together before working through your group members' respective questions. This way you can review and discuss the content you found important before working through the questions. Remember, your role as the leader is to facilitate a dialogue, not preach a sermon.

Tip 2: There is a lot of reading in this chapter, but don't be intimidated. Take your time to read through the chart and the brief section on the life of Athanasius. This is your history, so spend a considerable amount of time with your group in these sections. Consider also how the stories of the Early African Church Fathers and Mothers debunk the idea that we were an illiterate, uneducated people before slavery in America.

Chapter Three

EARLY AFRICAN CHRISTIANITY

I. The Ethiopian Eunuch Revisited

In the previous chapter, we took a brief look at the story of the Ethiopian eunuch. This story is significant because it helps overturn the lie that Christianity is a white man's religion, but also because it marks the initial fulfillment of Jesus's promise in Acts 1:8. Let's take a closer look.

Just before Jesus ascended into the heavens, He promised His disciples, "You will receive power when the Holy Spirit comes upon you. And you will be my witnesses, telling people about me everywhere—in Jerusalem, throughout Judea, in Samaria, and to the ends of the earth" (Acts 1:8).

If you were to do a quick survey of the first eight chapters of the Book of Acts, you would find the story of how the gospel quickly moved from Jerusalem to the uttermost parts of the earth. In Acts 2, after the Spirit came down and filled the disciples who were gathered in the city of Jerusalem, 3,000 people were saved (Acts 2:41)! Later in Acts 4:4, we are told that their numbers in Jerusalem grew from 3,000 to 5,000. In Acts 8, due to persecution, Christians were scattered throughout Judea and Samaria (Acts 8:1). But that didn't keep them for talking about Jesus. Instead, "the believers who were scattered preached the Good News about Jesus wherever they went" (Acts 8:4). The gospel was on the move, and as more people were filled with the Holy Spirit, new witnesses were born.

Then we come to the story of the Ethiopian eunuch. Philip, a deacon of the church in Jerusalem, was instructed by an angel of the Lord to leave Samaria and travel south to a desert road that went from Jerusalem to Gaza. *What kind of evangelistic work could possibly be found on this desert road?* Hardly anyone traveled on it. There were no villages or towns surrounding it.

Upon his arrival, Philip found a single chariot traveling along the road. He ran over to catch up with it at the Spirit's prompting. As he got close to the chariot, he heard a man reading from the scroll of Isaiah. Philip realized he was Ethiopian, not Jewish, and asked, "Do you understand what you are reading?"

Though the Ethiopian eunuch had likely traveled from Ethiopia to Jerusalem to worship God at a Jewish festival, he had no idea what or who Isaiah was talking about. All he knew was that God was real and deserving of his devotion. He believed this so much that he traveled five-and-a-half months to worship God at a temple he wouldn't even be able to set foot in. By Jewish law, the Ethiopian eunuch was prevented from entering the temple because he was a foreigner. And not only that, but his status as a eunuch also prevented him from worshipping in the temple because he was considered unclean by Jewish law (Exodus 12:34; Deuteronomy 23:1; Ezekiel 44:6-9). All he could do was stand outside the temple and listen as people raised their voices to God.

So, out of an eagerness to know the God he had just traveled to worship, he gladly welcomes Philip aboard his chariot to explain. Philip picks up from where the Ethiopian eunuch was reading in Isaiah 53:7-8 and begins to share the gospel. Imagine how the Ethiopian eunuch's heart fluttered when they got to Isaiah 56:3-8:

> For this is what the Lord says:
> I will bless those eunuchs
> who keep my Sabbath days holy
> and who choose to do what pleases me
> and commit their lives to me.
>
> I will give them—within the walls of my house—
> a memorial and a name
> far greater than sons and daughters could give.

For the name I give them is an everlasting one.
It will never disappear!

I will also bless the foreigners who commit themselves to the Lord,
who serve him and love his name,
who worship him and do not desecrate the Sabbath day of rest,
and who hold fast to my covenant.

I will bring them to my holy mountain of Jerusalem
and will fill them with joy in my house of prayer.
I will accept their burnt offerings and sacrifices,
because my Temple will be called a house of prayer for all nations.

How do you think these words landed on the heart of the Ethiopian eunuch? How might these words have changed his understanding of God and himself?

With this renewed perspective of God and himself, along with an understanding of Christ's role in his salvation, the Ethiopian eunuch realizes every barrier to God had been torn down. In Christ, he is no longer a foreigner, but a son. In Christ, he is no longer unclean, but clean. This is why, when the Ethiopian eunuch saw a pool of water, he asked Philip if there was anything preventing him from being baptized (Acts 8:36). Seeing that there was nothing standing in the man's way, Philip baptized him.

What a gift! For the first time the Ethiopian eunuch was able to participate in worship and obedience to the Lord just like everyone other Christian!

Given this review of Acts 1-8, consider the question below, which was posed in the last chapter. "Is Christianity a white man's religion?" What might you add to your response?

Why would God call Philip away from a successful ministry to go to a desert road to meet the Ethiopian eunuch?

The Holy Spirit didn't just send Philip to that deserted road to reveal God's desire for "burnt-faced" people to know Him. The Holy Spirit sent Philip to that deserted road to fulfill Jesus's promise to empower His people to be witnesses to the ends of the earth.

In his commentary on the book of Acts, biblical scholar F.F. Bruce writes, "The Ethiopians were regarded by the Greeks and their neighbors . . . as living on the edge of the world."[16] If this is true, it means that Luke is intentionally sharing the story of the Ethiopian Eunuch to show that his conversion is the initial fulfillment of Jesus's promise in Acts 1:8 to reach the world.

The conversion of Ethiopian eunuch—a "burnt-faced" black man—is the first fruits of Jesus's promise for His disciples to take the gospel to the uttermost parts of the earth. This is incredible!

If God intentionally inspired the writers of Scripture to record particular stories, then who they were, in regard to their ethnicity, gender, and socio-economic status, mattered. Why is it significant that the first non-Jew to receive Christ was a black man? What significance does this have for the church? What significance does this have for you, personally?

The end of the Ethiopian eunuch's story says, "he went on his way rejoicing" (Acts 8:39). Though Luke doesn't tell us what happens when he gets back home to Ethiopia, it's not totally a mystery. The man's heart was bursting with joy!

16. F.F. Bruce, The Book of Acts (Grand Rapids, MI: Eerdmans Publishing Company), 178-9.

In 2 Corinthians 5:14-15, Paul writes, "For the love of Christ compels us, since we have reached this conclusion: If one died for all, then all died. And he died so that those who live should no longer live for themselves, but for the one who died for them and was raised" (CSB). The word "compel" can be likened to being forced into a corner. When you are forced into a corner, you feel suffocated, stuck; like your only option is to surrender to your opponent. Sounds awful, right? Why would Paul use such an awful analogy to describe Christ's love? Paul is taking this concept and spinning it on its head to explain the inescapable, irresistible, all-consuming love of God. Because Paul experienced God's love in his life, he couldn't help but surrender it and share it with others. The same was true for the Ethiopian eunuch.

II. Going Deeper

Read 2 Corinthians 5:14–21. Use the five-step process for Bible study presented in chapter one to unwrap the meaning of this passage and its implications for those in Christ, then answer the following questions.

- Share with one another how God saved and captured you with His love.
- How does Christ's love compel you to die to yourself and live for Him?
- What does it mean to be a "new creation" according to this text?
- According to this text, what does it mean to be an "ambassador of Christ"?
- If gaining the identity of an ambassador for Christ is a natural consequence for all who place their faith in Jesus, what do you think the Ethiopian eunuch did when he got home? How might he have leveraged his position as an officer to the Queen for God's glory?

Dr. David Daniels, who has done extensive research in the area of Church History, shares the following about the church in Ethiopia:[17]

- The church of Ethiopia was firmly established during the first century. This is within the first 100 years of Christ's ascension.
- Ethiopia was the first kingdom to accept Christianity as its state religion.
- During the sixteenth century, Ethiopia was commended by Martin Luther,

17. David Daniels, "The African Roots of the Reformation" [Audio podcast]. Retrieved from https://podcasts.apple.com/us/podcast/african-roots-reformation-special-guest-dr-david-daniels/id978012810?i=1000394480912. The Jude 3 Project (November 2017).

> the father of the Reformation, for not wavering from the faith. Unlike the church at Rome, they had not added unbiblical rules that prevented people from experiencing the grace of the gospel. (If you don't know much about Martin Luther and the Reformation, a church being commended by Luther is like a basketball player being commended by Michael Jordan; they both have high standards and are not quick to hand out compliments.)

By God's grace the whole kingdom of Ethiopia was reached with the gospel. And not only Ethiopia, but by God's grace other countries in Africa were reached. Within the first 100 years of Christianity, churches were established in Egypt.[18] By the fifth century, churches began to pop up in Nubia, which led to its Christianization in the year 543.[19]

In the opening pages of *How Africa Shaped the Christian Mind*, our white chocolate brother, Dr. Thomas C. Oden writes,

> "Africa played a decisive role in the formation of Christian culture. Decisive intellectual achievements of Christianity were explored and understood first in Africa before they were recognized in Europe, and a millennium before they found their way to North America."[20]

Africa set the standard for academia, hermeneutics, the formulation of Church doctrine, and so much more. You can't go to a seminary, preach a sermon, or talk about the nature of Christ without bumping up against the influence of the Early African church.

AFRICAN CHURCH LEADERS AND THE CONTRIBUTIONS TO THE CHURCH

Clement of Alexandria (c. 169–215)
Location: Alexandria
Role: Presbyter (Elder)

---

18. Everett Ferguson, Church History, Volume One: From Christ to the Pre-Reformation (Grand Rapids, Michigan: Zondervan, 2013), 8.

19. Ibid., 30.

20. Thomas C. Oden, How Africa Shaped the Christian Mind: Rediscovering the African Seedbed of Western Christianity (Downers Grove, IL: InterVarsity Press, 2007), 9.

Contribution: Clement was an apologist. He was always looking for ways to integrate his faith with the world around him. He had a gift for utilizing philosophy to explain the truths and implication of God's word with those who were far from God. One of his greatest works is a book called *The Instructor*, which was the first literary work on Christian ethics. It presented Jesus as the divine Logos (Word) that instructs the Christian on how to live in society.[21] Pastors, theologians, and apologists still use Clement's methods as a way to build a bridge from doubt to faith.

Tertullian (c. 160–220)
Location: Carthage
Role: Christian Writer
Contribution: Tertullian was a complicated brother. If you take a listen to our Jude 3 podcast "Tertullian: The Good, Bad, & Ugly," you'll learn why. However, the Church is forever indebted to Tertullian for his work on the three-person nature of God. Tertullian coined the term "Trinity," along with many others like "original sin" and "sacrament," to help the early Church make sense of their faith.[22]

Saint Perpetua (c. 182–203)
Location: Carthage
Role: Martyr
Contribution: Perpetua was a 22-year-old mother who refused to obey the Roman emperor and renounce her faith in Jesus Christ. Though her father urged her to be sensible, she endured imprisonment, torture, and death for the sake of the gospel. In the days leading up to her death, she not only nourished the church with her bravery and commitment to endure against persecution, but she also nourished her infant by nursing him while in prison. Perpetua contended for the faith until death.

Saint Felicitas (c. ?–203)
Location: Carthage
Role: Martyr
Contribution: Felicitas was a bad mamma jamma! Even though she was pregnant, she refused to obey the emperor and renounce her faith in Jesus Christ. Along with Perpetua's, her commitment to Christ in the midst of motherhood spoke volumes to the persecuted church at Carthage. Felicitas gave birth to her baby girl just days before her execution. As she cried out in pain during childbirth, someone asked her, "How are you ever going to endure the suffering of martyrdom?" Felicitas replied,

---

21. Ferguson, 129.

22. Ibid., 126.

"Now it is I who suffer what I am suffering; then, there will be Another in me Who will suffer for me, because I will be suffering for Him."[23]

Origen (c. 185–251)
Location: Alexandria
Role: Christian Writer
Contributions: Though Origen is often criticized for being on the edge of orthodoxy, he gave the Church a blueprint for how to properly study God's Word (hermeneutics). He, along with Clement of Alexandria and Tertullian, was the first to use the term "New Testament" or "New Covenant" as a way to establish which books should be recognized as authoritative Scripture.[24]

Augustine of Hippo (c. 354–430)
Location: North Africa
Role: Presbyter (Elder)
Contributions: Augustine is the G.O.A.T when it comes to theologians. He has shaped much of the way we think about Church and its function in the world, along with the way the we understand the roles of grace and free will in one's salvation. His most famous quote—"You have made us for yourself, O Lord, and our hearts are restless until they rest in you"—is still used by many pastors, writes, and singers as a way to encourage the Church to turn from its idols.

Given what you have learned about the Ethiopian church and these African Church Fathers, make a list of the ways in which their contributions are currently influencing the church.

III. Athanasius: The Jude 3 Prototype

Another prominent African Church Father is Athanasius of Alexandria (c. 296–373). Though much has not been written about the early years of his life, Dr. John Tyson recounts an endearing story of how Athanasius was caught by the Bishop of

23. https://www.loyolapress.com/our-catholic-faith/saints/saints-stories-for-all-ages/saint-perpetua-and-saint-felicity

24. Ferguson, 115.

Alexandria playing church with his friends.[25] He preached a full sermon and even performed a few baptisms. (Yep, black folks been "playing church" since the third century.)

However, when the Bishop of Alexandria questioned Athanasius's actions, he realized Athanasius wasn't playing church at all. The Bishop was so convinced by this that he confirmed the baptisms Athanasius had administered and took him under his wing to train him for ministry.

Though Athanasius was often overlooked because of his youth and small stature, he became a strong yet humble force in the church at Alexandria. During the first few centuries of Christianity, there were some in the church that found it difficult to understand that Jesus was both fully God and fully human. They struggled with this idea for two reasons:

1. Monotheism, the belief that there is only one God, is a central belief of the Jewish faith. Some believed that if they accepted Jesus as God, they were deviating from monotheism and taking up polytheism. Polytheism, the belief in multiple gods, was a pagan belief that no Christian or Jew wanted to be associated with.
2. Many found it difficult to conceptualize how Jesus could be fully God and fully human. How was it possible for His divinity to co-exist within His humanity?

Deep questions, right? Fair questions, too. However, some allowed their questions to lead them to unfortunate heresies. One of these heresies was Arianism. Arian, a presbyter and popular preacher in the church at Alexandria, got around the complexities concerning the nature of Jesus by suggesting "there was (once) a time when Jesus was not."[26] By this he meant that Jesus was the created son of God who was God's instrument in the creation of the world.[27] This interpretation allowed Arius to hold onto his monotheistic beliefs while affirming Jesus's divinity. That would mean Jesus was not co-eternal or co-equal with the Father and the Holy Spirit, and would make Jesus subordinate to God, the Father.

---

25. John Tyson, "The Life and Work of Athanasius" [Audio podcast]. Retreived from https://podcasts.apple.com/us/podcast/the-life-and-work-of-athanasius-special-guest-dr-john-tyson/id978012810?i=1000390911456. The Jude 3 Project (August 2017)

26. Ferguson, 192.

27. Ibid., 192.

On the surface, this may seem like a minor or even insignificant deviation, but in Athanasius's mind, to strip Jesus of even once ounce of His divinity was to strip Him of His ability to save the world. In his book *On the Incarnation*, Athanasius passionately argues,

> For the Word (Jesus), realizing that in no other way would the corruption of human beings be undone except, simply, by dying, yet being immortal and the Son of the Father the Word was not able to die, for this reason he takes to Himself a body capable of death, in order that it, participating in the Word who is above all, might be sufficient for death on behalf of all, and through the indwelling Word would remain incorruptible, and so corruption might henceforth cease from all by the grace of the resurrection. Whence, by offering to death the body he had taken to Himself, as an offering holy and free of all spot, he immediately abolished death from all like Him. . . . For being above all, the Word of God consequently, by offering His own temple and His bodily instrument as a substitute for all, fulfilled in death that which was required. . . . And now the very corruption of death no longer holds ground against human beings because of the (the Word that became flesh).[28]

If that was easy for you to read, God bless you! If not, that's understandable—this is a fourth century writing that was originally written in Latin and was translated to English in 1944. There are a lot of layers that prevent us from being able to catch the meaning of Athanasius's words in just one reading.

Take a moment to read this excerpt again. Once you get a sense of what Athanasius is saying, try to create a summary for yourself in the space provided below.

____

____

____

IV. Summary

For Athanasius, contending against the heresy of Arianism was not a matter of being right; it was a matter of preserving the beauty and glory of the God who came down

28. Athanasius & C. S. Lewis, On the incarnation: The Treatise De Incarnatione Verbi Dei (Crestwood, NY: St. Vladimirs Seminary Press, 2003), 58.

and put on flesh to provide salvation for all who put their trust in Him. If Christ were not fully human and fully divine, there would be no hope for us to be fully saved and renewed. The Incarnation—Jesus's coming in the flesh—was necessary. Athanasius is known for summarizing it this way: "He became what we are so that we might become who is."

During his lifetime, Athanasius would experience many highs and lows as he contended for the Incarnation of Christ. One of those highs would be at the Council of Nicaea in 325. Due to the growing tensions in the Church concerning the nature of Christ, the Roman emperor Constantine called for church leaders throughout the empire to gather in Nicaea to reach an agreement on the matter.

At the gathering, Athanasius and others called for the council to "do away with the irreligious phrases of the Arians" that taught Christ did not always exist and was born before the creation of the world.[29] Because of their due diligence, Arianism was denied and a creed (statement of faith) was drafted to protect the Church from further heresies. Many have said that if it were not for Athanasius "the church would have probably fallen into the hands of the Arians."[30]

Though this is high praise for Athanasius, his commitment to contend against heresy did not come without a cost. After Constantine's the death, questions concerning the nature of Christ resurfaced. This would result in Athanasius being exiled a total of five times because of his unwillingness to waver in the matter.

At the Jude 3 Project, our objectives are two-fold: (1) To help the Christian community know what they believe and why they believe it; (2) to equip believers to contend for the faith for the glory of God.

In what ways do you see Athanasius live out these objectives in his own life?
How does Athanasius's life encourage you?

---

29. Nicene and Post-Nicene Fathers, Second Series, Volume 4, Athanasius: Select Works and Letters (Grand Rapids, MI: Hendrickson, 1995), 126.

30. Ibid, 306.

ONE MORE THING . . .

Remember our white chocolate brother, Thomas Oden, who was mentioned earlier in this chapter? He writes, "Ordinary African Christian believers deserve to have a much more accessible way understanding early African Christianity: its faith, courage, tenacity and remarkable intellectual strength . . . this story must be told."

He's right. The story of the Early African Church must be told. But whose responsibility is it to tell?

Dr. Vince Bantu explains that many people have come to reject Christianity not because they have issues with Jesus, but because they primarily associate Christianity with colonialism and slavery. But this is simply because they haven't gone back far enough into history to learn the whole story.

> "We . . . have to go back and reeducate our people and our community . . . and also to help people understand the last five centuries that we have experienced are not the beginning of the story. . . if someone was only to look at the last five centuries, then it (Christianity) would seem like it's the white man's religion and it's a mechanism of oppression. But, when you go back 500 years or a 1,000 more years and you go back to the early church then you find out that Christianity was growing in Africa before it was ever growing in Europe. When Europeans were still worshipping Oden and Thor, African Christians in Egypt, North Africa, Ethiopia, and Nubia were worshipping Jesus as Lord and Savior before Islam even existed."[31]

Now, this is not an attempt to throw shade at our European brothers and sisters. The same blood that was shed for us was shed for them. We don't possess a higher place in the kingdom over them. But the little bit of evidence presented in this chapter undermines the idea that Christianity is a white man's religion, or that if it weren't for slavery, black people wouldn't have ever heard the gospel. These statements are ignorant, uneducated, and simply untrue.

Brothers and sisters, in order for us to competently contend for the faith against these lies, we must know our history. Our Early African Church History. What are you going to do?

---

31. Vince Bantu, "Is Christianity a White Man's Religion?", [Audio podcast] Retrieved from http://www.jude3project.com/podcast/whitemansreligion?rq=vince%20bantu. The Jude 3 Project (June 2016)

What are one to two ways you have been impacted by what you've learned in this chapter?

Identify one person or topic from this chapter you would like to study further. Who can you invite to study it with you?

V. Tools for Going Deeper

- Athanasius & C. S. Lewis, On the Incarnation: The Treatise De Incarnatione Verbi Dei (Crestwood, NY: St. Vladimirs Seminary Press, 2003).
- Bengt Sundkler and Christopher Steed, A History of the Church in Africa (New York, NY: Cambridge University Press, 2000).
- Everett Ferguson, Church History, Volume One: From Christ to the Pre-Reformation (Grand Rapids, Michigan: Zondervan, 2013).
- Thomas C. Oden, How Africa Shaped the Christian Mind: Rediscovering the African Seedbed of Western Christianity (Downers Grove, IL: InterVarsity Press, 2007).
- Visit throughcoloredeyes.com for more.

Leader's Guide

CHAPTER FOUR

Objective

To highlight the many contributions of black churches.

Big Ideas

1. When you look at the black church as an institution, it has no match and no equal as it pertains to institutions that have brought tangible resources to the black community. "For more than 300 years, black churches have been providing support in the way of mutual aid, legislative advocacy, training ground, professional development . . . [more] than any other of the wonderful organizations that work on behalf of or in the midst of the black community. The Black Church has no equal and no rival in the way of producing concrete and material supports…it has created lasting results for more than three centuries." —Dr. Heber Brown, "Food Justice" (Jude 3 Podcast)

2. Black churches brought about lasting change because of the Spirit-filled men and women who comprised it. It was their deep abiding faith in Jesus Christ that compelled them to live generously, sacrificially, and intentionally for the sake of others. Before these men and women were activists, they were followers of Jesus Christ.

3. It will only be our deep abiding faith in Jesus Christ that will compel us to live generously, sacrificially, and intentionally for the sake of others. The same biblical convictions that propelled the past generation of men and women to fight against injustice will need to become our own. Our biblical convictions are the only way we will persevere in speaking out against injustice and bringing about change.

JUDE 3 PROJECT

Podcast Playlist

"The Black Church and Economic Development"
Guest: Bishop Vaughn McCaughlin
Date: March 2017

"Food Justice"
Guest: Dr. Heber Brown
Date: April 2018

Helpful Tips

Tip 1: Select the paragraphs and sections you would like to read together before working through your group's questions. This way you can review and discuss the content you found important before working through the questions.

Tip 2: Don't miss that before these men and women were activists, they were Christians. They were people of conviction. They weren't just woke for the sake of being woke. Fighting against injustice wasn't trendy. It was bloody. The only thing that kept them going was the vision that God laid out in Scripture for every person to be treated as those who were created in His image. Before it was Martin's dream, it was God's! Pray as a group that your pursuit of justice would be motivated by God's heart for the world.

Chapter Four

CONTRIBUTIONS OF BLACK CHURCHES

I. Is "The Black Church" Dead?

On April 26, 2010 at 5:12 a.m., Dr. Eddie Glaude, Jr., the professor of religion and chair of the center for African American Studies at Princeton University, pronounced the Black Church dead.[32]

Do you agree with Glaude's pronouncement? Why or why not?

Glaude said the Black Church was dead for four reasons:

1. It has allowed its conservatism to prevent it from being on the forefront of today's political issues.
2. It presumes its ongoing relevance because of its past good works and reputation.

32. Eddie Glaude, The Black Church is Dead, Retrieved May 30, 2019 from https://www.huffpost.com/entry/the-black-church-is-dead_b_473815?guccounter=1.

3. It's no longer the center of black life as a moral and social compass.
4. It has lost its prophetic voice on the national stage.

ARE BLACK CHURCHES' GLORY DAYS BEHIND US? DO BLACK CHURCHES HAVE ANYTHING LEFT TO OFFER?

In this chapter, we will look at the past and present contributions of black churches while also considering its future.

II. The Past Contributions of Black Churches

When asked "Why the Black Church?" concerning his work with The Black Church Food Security Network, Rev. Dr. Heber Brown responded,

> When you look at the Black Church as an institution, it has no match and no equal as it pertains to institutions that have brought tangible resources to the black community. For more than 300 years, black churches have been providing support in the way of mutual aid, legislative advocacy, training ground, professional development . . . [more] than any other of the wonderful organizations that work on behalf of or in the midst of the black community. The Black Church has no equal and no rival in the way of producing concrete and material supports...it has created lasting results for more than three centuries.[33]

Did you that know many Historically Black Colleges and Universities (HBCUs) were founded by black churches and denominations? Howard University was founded in 1866 by a band of African-American missionaries to provide theological education to African-American pastors and preachers.[34] In 1867, Morehouse was founded in the basement of Springfield Baptist Church in Augusta, GA.[35] The list goes on:

33. Heber Brown, "Food Justice" [Audio podcast]. Retrieved from https://podcasts.apple.com/us/podcast/food-justice-special-guest-dr-heber-brown/id978012810?i=1000408246683 Jude 3 Project (April 2018).

34. Erica Taylor, Little Known Black History Fact: Howard University, Retrieved May 30, 2019 from https://blackamericaweb.com/2013/12/18/little-known-black-history-fact-howard-university/

35. Morehouse Legacy, Retrieved May 30, 2019 from https://www.morehouse.edu/about/legacy.html

North Carolina Central University in Durham, NC, Oakwood University in Huntsville, AL, Xavier University of Louisiana in New Orleans, LA.

When African-Americans had little to no access to financial resources due to slavery and discrimination, black churches pulled their resources together to ensure each person had what they needed for life and upward mobility. In 1787, during slavery, two local pastors named Richard Allen and Absalom Jones founded the Free African Society (FAS). The society's main goal was to provide aid to newly freed blacks so that they could gather strength and develop leaders in the community.[36] And get this—the FAS was funded by benevolence offerings and donations from other black people trying to foster stability and upward mobility in their own lives. Imagine the relief and encouragement the FAS provided to newly freed slaves who owned nothing and likely found it difficult to find jobs because white folks preferred free labor over paying for it.

Black churches also gave birth to several credit unions to provide housing and educational loans to African-Americans during the Jim Crow era. In his podcast interview, Dr. Marvin L. McMickle shared that Antioch Baptist Church founded its own credit union in 1945 as a means to provide loans to African-American soldiers who couldn't get conventional mortgages from any other banks in Cleveland, OH.[37] These men fought in World War II for the freedom of every yellow, red, black and white American, but they couldn't get a loan in the country for which they had risked their life. Several other black churches around the country organized credit unions to ensure black people were treated with dignity and respect.

We could go on and on about the past contributions of black churches. Have you heard of the Civil Rights Movement? Are you familiar with march at Selma? Are you aware the NAACP conducted most of their business in the pews of black churches? Do you know the where black people in the time of slavery and Jim Crow found refuge in times of despair and trouble? Are you familiar with the songs that they sung? Much of our current freedom is indebted to black churches.

---

36. The Free African Society, Retrieved May 30, 2019 fromhttps://hsp.org/history-online/exhibits/richard-allen-apostle-of-freedom/the-free-african-society

37. Marvin McMickle, "Contributions of the Black Church" [Youtube Video] Retrieved May 31, 2019 from https://www.youtube.com/watch?v=5jSe1o4GEcA

What are some other past contributions of black churches?

Black churches brought about lasting change because of the Spirit-filled men and women who comprised it. In *An Encyclopedia of African American Christian Heritage*, Dr. McMickle records stories of how these ordinary men and women lived out their faith in an extraordinary God. His book is not only a gift to black churches, but to the church as a whole, as it chronicles a part of church history that is often ignored or overlooked. Here are a few of the Jude 3 Project's favorites from his book, along with a few from other sources:

Richard Allen (1760–1831) is an impressive man. In 1786, Allen purchased his freedom along with that of his wife and children through a process called gradual manumission. One year later, Allen co-founded the Free African Society for the economic and leadership development of recently freed slaves (mentioned above). He was a congregant at St. George Methodist Church in Philadelphia, PA, where his role was to preach to black congregants. However, after he and other black worshippers were removed from a prayer meeting for praying in the "white only" section, they left. This episode of discrimination led to his founding of Bethel Church and African Methodist Episcopal (AME) Church—the first black denomination in America. And—don't miss this—it was founded during slavery! Allen was not only a devoted clergyman but also a savvy businessman. "After purchasing his freedom and that of his wife, he owned and operated several businesses in Philadelphia; his enterprises included a blacksmith shop, shoemaking, and chimney sweeping. Upon his death, he left his family an estate valued at $80,000."[38]

Charles Octavius Boothe (1845–1924) is a true gift to black churches. Before there was the Civil Rights Movement, there was Charles Octavius Boothe at the helm of the Racial Uplift. Before there was Dr. Martin Luther King, Jr. at Dexter Avenue Baptist church (now King's Memorial Baptist Church), there was its founder Charles Octavius Boothe. Through the Racial Uplift, Boothe "worked to improve

38. Marvin McMickle, The Encyclopedia of African American Christian Heritage, (King of Prussia, PA: Judson Press 2002), 3.

the spiritual, social, and intellectual well-being of African-Americans in a society that denied their humanity before God and its Constitution."[39] In 1890, thirty-five years after the Emancipation Proclamation, Boothe wrote and published a systematic theology called *A Plain Theology for Plain People.* Boothe penned this resource out of a desire to equip the saints for the work of ministry so that each of them would reach maturity in Christ despite their lack of formal education. In his mind, it was their birthright to have access to a deep and vibrant understanding of the triune God. He writes, "The private members of churches who have but little time for books, but have great need for the truths that teach, should find the truth suited to their time, their understanding, and their wants. Indeed, our hope lies in the religious education of the whole people."[40]

James Cone (1940–2018) is likely one of the most controversial theologians of the twentieth century. However, he is beloved and revered by many because he called for white theologians, professors, and pastors to address the sufferings of black folks in their teaching and theology. After receiving his Ph.D. in systematic theology from Northwestern, Cone went on to teach at Philander Smith (HBCU), Adrian College, and Union Theological Seminary. "At Union he laid out the arguments and created much of the bibliography for black theology, beginning with [his books] *Black Theology and Black Power, A Black Theology of Liberation,* and *God of the Oppressed.*"[41] His writings and outcry for the liberation of black folks earned him the title "father of liberation theology." Cone's work has been used by many other minority groups to develop a theology that addresses their suffering while also calling for their liberation.

Jerena Lee (1783–1855) is the first black woman to be recognized as a preacher. After several years of wrestling with her flesh and depression, she came to faith in Jesus Christ under the preaching of Richard Allen. In 1807, Lee "heard the voice of God commissioning her to preach."[42] Lee shared her call to preach with Allen but was turned away because there wasn't anything in the AME's bylaws that would allow her to preach. Lee responded to this technicality with, "O how careful ought we to be, lest through our bylaws of church government and discipline, we bring into disrepute even the word of life. For [how] unseemingly . . . [is it] for a woman to

39. Charles Octavius Boothe, A Plain Theology for a Plain People, (Bellingham, WA: Lexham Press), viii.

40. Ibid, 3.

41. McMickle, 95.

42. Teisha Wilsion, Jarena Lee, Retrieved May 31, 2019 from https://www.blackpast.org/african-american-history/lee-jarena-1783/

preach, seeing the Savior died for the woman as well as the man?"[43] It wouldn't be until thirteen years later that Lee would be allowed to preach. But once one door was open for her, God opened several more. Lee was the first African American woman to publicly preach to "racially mixed Methodists, Presbyterian, Baptist, and Wesleyan audiences across the Mid-Atlantic states, lower Canada, Cincinnati, Detroit, and New England."[44] Lee paved the way for women in ministry in the AME church and the church at large, which is why *Christianity Today* named her a "trailblazer for women in ministry."

Rebecca Protten (1718–1780) is exalted by many scholars as the "mother of modern missions."[45] Upon receiving her freedom from her slave owners at the age of twelve, Protten resolved to use her freedom as a means to preach what she called "the liberating gospel of grace" to those who remained enslaved. As a teenager she faithfully entered into slave quarters located in the plantations of St. Thomas to proclaim the gospel of salvation to domestic servants, cane boilers, weavers, and cotton pickers whose bodies and spirits were stripped every day by slavery.[46] She was a force. Hundreds—possibly even thousands—came to faith through her missionary efforts.[47] In the book *Rebecca's Revival: Creating Black Christianity in the Atlantic World*, Dr. Jon F. Sensbach reports that her ministry in the Caribbean became "one of the great social and religious movements of modern history, [as] black women and men began to blend Christianity with the religions they had brought with them from Africa, creating a faith to fortify themselves against slavery."[48]

J. Deotis Roberts (1927–) is a giant in the field of theology. Roberts envisions a liberation of black people that also brings about reconciliation. As a black man born in contentious North Carolina who has earned a bachelor of arts degree from Johnson C. Smith University (HBCU), a bachelors of divinity from Shaw University (HBCU), a doctor of philosophy degree from Edinburgh University in Scotland, and

43. McMickle, 71.

44. Eric Washington, Jarena Lee, Retrieved May 31, 2019 from https://www.christianitytoday.com/history/people/pastorsandpreachers/jarena-lee.html

45. Retrieved May 31, 2019 from https://en.wikipedia.org/wiki/Rebecca_Protten

46. Jon F. Sensbach, Rebecca's Revival: Creating Black Christianity in the Atlantic World, (Cambridge, MA: Harvard University Press), 4.

47. https://www.thegospelcoalition.org/article/meet-mother-of-modern-missions/ Retrieved May 31, 2019`

48. Sensbach, 5.

who has served as a professor at HBCUs like Howard University and predominately white institutions like Duke University, Roberts deeply yearns for reconciliation among all his brothers and sisters. He rubs shoulders with all kinds of people and desires for them all to live as though God had indeed torn down the dividing wall of hostility in Christ (Ephesians 2:14) His book, *Liberation and Reconciliation,* provides a biblical pathway for how God calls Christians are to engage in issues of systemic racism, justice, and reconciliation.

Which one of these stories stood out to you the most? What inspired you? How have these men and women encouraged you in your faith?

Which one of these black church leaders would you like to study further? If you are using this resource in a group, consider splitting up this list of leaders up among your group and doing more research on them. Plan to share your findings with one another the next time you meet.

Please do not miss that for each of these men and women it was their deep abiding faith in Jesus Christ that compelled them to live generously, sacrificially, and intentionally for the sake of others.

Richard Allen's and the Free African Society's acceptance of Acts 2:43–47 as the model for the church compelled them to generously give and share everything they had with one another. It was Rebecca Protten's belief that Christ "died for everyone so that those who received new life would no longer live for themselves" that compelled her to live sacrificially for the spiritual and bodily freedom of others (2 Corinthians 5:14–15). It was Charles Octavis Boothe's, Dr. James Cone's, and Dr. J, Deotis Roberts' conviction that every man and woman was created in the image of Christ that compelled them to intentionally labor for the theological education and liberation of others. Before these men and women were activists, they were followers of Jesus Christ.

It was their belief in a God whose justice would soon shine like the noonday sun that fueled their activism (Psalms 37:6).

III. The Present Contributions of Black Churches

Dr. Glaude wasn't lying when he suggested that black churches have a past that would be difficult to recreate. Though we understand his sentiments concerning the vitality of black churches and would agree with him on some points, we at the Jude 3 Project disagree that "the Black Church" is dead for the following reasons:

1. In his podcast interview, Dr. McMickle clarifies that Glaude pronounced the church dead out of a belief that "the Black Church as the central institution in the lives of black communities [is] coming to an end." Dr. McMickle wisely points out that this has less to do with the Black Church's vitality and more to do with the secularization of America. In 2009, the Barna Group, a research group that tracks spiritual and cultural trends in America, reported that only 9% of Americans had a biblical worldview. If that number doesn't shock you, maybe you would be surprised to know that this means only one out of every five of those who profess to be Christians have a biblical worldview. People are no longer looking to the church as their moral or social compass. However, as long as God's Spirit fills His church, she is alive and poised to do the work God has commissioned her to do (Act 1:8)! To pronounce her dead is a theological fallacy and irresponsible, even if you are simply speaking to the loss of her prophetic voice in the political sphere.[49]
2. Through much of our work at the Jude 3 Project, we have encountered a host of scholars, churches, and stories that testify to the vitality of black churches. In our episode, The Black Church and Economic Development, Bishop Vaughn McLaughlin shares the work that his church, Potter's House International Ministries, is doing for the social, educational, economical, and spiritual well-being of the people of Jacksonville, FL.[50] They have given birth to a fully accredit-

49. Eric Mason, Woke Church, Retrieved June 10, 2019 from https://podcasts.apple.com/us/podcast/woke-church-special-guest-dr-eric-mason/id978012810?i=1000422938068.

50. Vaughn McCaughlin , "The Black Church and Economic Development" [Audio Podcast]. Retrieved from https://podcasts.apple.com/us/podcast/black-church-economic-empowerment-special-guest-bishop/id978012810?i=1000382079366 Jude 3 Podcast (March 2017).

ed institution of academia that currently has over 600 students enrolled from grades K–4 to twelfth grade. Following in the footsteps of black church forefathers, they have started a federal credit union to provide the marginalized with loans for housing and financial upward mobility. They also have opened up a whole mall where they help many small businesses in their community get off to a good start by allowing them to use space in the mall rent free. This is a church that is making itself central to the life of its community. And it's not the only one! There are black churches all over the country doing this kind of work. But these are not the churches that receive media coverage. These are not the churches whose content floods our Instagram and Twitter feeds. We must be careful not to allow that which is viral to shape our understanding of reality. Just because something is viral, doesn't mean it's valid.[51]

3. Additionally, many of our podcast guests are standing on the frontlines of bringing spiritual renewal, economic empowerment, and social flourishing to black communities around the country. There's Dr. Heber Brown and his work to ensure marginalized communities have access to quality food. There's Pastor Jerome Gay and his diligence to expose the lies of black cults such as Hebrew Israelites and Pan-Africanism. There's Michelle Higgins, Dr. Christina Edmundson, and Ekemini Uwan, who with a balance of theological depth, cultural relevance, and sass on their podcast, Truth's Table, speak up against issues of injustice and racism as a way to empower women (and men) to live as people who are truly free. There's Dr. Vince Bantu and his impeccable historical research to ensure that black people know the truth about Christianity and its African origins. And there's Dr. Tiffany Gill and her work to dismantle the lie that Christianity is a white man's religion through a brilliant presentation of African-American history.

Black churches are not dead! These churches are alive, and God has gifted them with an arsenal of leaders to continue to carry their influence forward for His glory.

IV. The Future Contributions of Black Churches

Black churches have brought about lasting change because of the men and women who comprised it and their faith in the God of the Bible. For our churches to continue

51. [@thejude3project]. (2019, May 28). You can't believe everything you read online [Instagram photograph]. Retrieved from https://www.instagram.com/p/ByAm1wGFhuZ.

bringing about lasting change, it will require men and women like you to grab ahold of the truths of the Bible in a way that propels God's vision for the world and His people forward. In his podcast interview, Dr. Mika Edmondson gives a profound answer to the question, "How should people and churches engage with issues of injustice?"

> I would say first and foremost to ask the Lord to help you understand what the gospel has to do with social justice and the pursuit of justice in the world, because if a Christian approaches these things outside of their faith or as an aside to the faith, then they won't really have the fortitude and the faith and the hope to continue in this work. If you don't understand that this is something that Christ has called us to and that Christ gives us the resources to pursue it, then you'll never truly sacrifice for it. You'll only be in it so far as it benefits you personally, and you won't really give yourself fully to it. So I would say Christians got to dig into the scriptures and into resources that help illuminate what the scriptures . . . have to say to issues of social injustice.

It was Scripture that fortified the efforts of Martin Luther King, Jr., Sojourner Truth, Harriet Tubman, and the host of other people mentioned in this chapter. It was their faith in the God of the scriptures that gave black churches their life. And it will be the same scriptures that awaken our generation and ensure the vitality of black churches in the future.

How does the gospel shape your understanding of social justice?

What passages of Scripture compel you to confront instances of racism and injustice? What passages of Scripture give you hope in the face of these challenges?

Brothers and sisters, the question isn't "Is the Black Church dead?" The question is, "Will God's people continue to rise up to proclaim, live out, and call the world around them to live out the truths of God's Word?" For us to contend for the faith in the face of secularism and the rise of black cults, we have to know what we believe and why we believe it. And this isn't just so we can win a debate or be classified as "woke." This is so we will persevere in our pursuit of bringing God's Kingdom down to earth as it is in heaven. We've got to be informed and inspired by God's vision for the world.

What are some practical ways you can grow in your knowledge of God's Word?

What is one thing in the African American community that burdens you? What passages of Scripture speak to that need?

How has God uniquely gifted you to be a blessing to your community?

How is your church currently being a blessing to your community? What other needs might your church be in a position to meet?

V. Tools for Going Deeper

- Charles Octavius Boothe, A Plain Theology for a Plain People, (Bellingham, WA: Lexham Press).
- James Cone, A Black Theology of Liberation, (Maryknoll, NY: Orbis Books, 1986).
- Marvin McMickle, The Encyclopedia of African American Christian Heritage, (King of Prussia, PA: Judson Press 2002).
- J. Deotis Roberts, Liberation and Reconciliation: A Black Theology, (Philadelphia, PA: Westminster Press, 1971).
- Jon F. Sensbach, Rebecca's Revival: Creating Black Christianity in the Atlantic World, (Cambridge, MA: Harvard University Press).

Leader's Guide

CHAPTER FIVE

Objective

To make participants aware of the major black cults and black ideologies and explain why many people are drawn to them.

Big Ideas

1. Black churches aren't perfect. After last week, it might be easy for you to go "all good" on black churches. However, like most things in this world, black churches are a mix of good and bad. And as you know, sometimes it comes with a little bit of ugly. These are things we need to be aware of in order to provide an apology for Christianity in a thoughtful and comprehensive way. We need to be prepared to contend for the faith when people call out the hypocrisy and bad theology that plague black churches.

2. Black churches are part of global family of God and are tied to the history of the American Church. As much as we want to distance ourselves from the history of the American Church, we are wedded to it both through its leaders' and followers' professions of faith in Jesus Christ. Because the American church was the backbone of American slavery, we need to be prepared to give an answer for the hope we have found in Christianity.

3. People's rejection of Christianity is justifiable given American history. Christians have done some horrible things. The pain some Christians have caused is real. We can't gloss over this. Instead, we need to slow down, share in people's sorrow, and ask good questions.

4. The formation of black cults is a way people have sought to deal with the Problem of Evil. The Problem of Evil asks the question, "If God is good and all powerful, why do bad things happen?" Some have concluded that because bad things happen, God must not exist, but black cults have taken a different approach. To hold onto their belief in a good God, they have manipulated the biblical narrative to explain why bad things have happened to black people and how God will redeem them in the end.

Podcast Playlist

"The Theology of Umar Johnson"
Guest: Pastor Jerome Gay
Date: November 2016

"The Truth About the American Church's Complicity in Racism"
Guest: Dr. Jemar Tisby
Date: January 2019

"Hebrew Israelites, KJV, & Black Identity"
Guest: Dr. Jamal Hopkins
Date: January 2019

Helpful Tips

Tip 1: Per usual, select the sections you would like to read together before working through your group member's respective questions.

Tip 2: A lot of information is covered in this chapter. Please take some time to listen to the podcasts listed above. They will greatly serve your preparation. This chapter will generate a lot of questions from your group. Do your best to keep them on track by avoiding tangents. Here are some statements you can make to keep you on track:

- "Kiesha, that's a really good question. However, I'm not sure if we have enough time to work through that question in a way that would do it justice. Can we hold that off until the end? If we have enough time, we can discuss it then."
- "Wow. Terrell, that's a really dope story about your friend. I want to hear more about that. Can we revisit that when we finish up?"
- In both of these cases, be sure to double back to their question or story. If you run out of time and can't revisit it, try to get some time with them the upcoming week or make some time in your next meeting to address it. Also, when you encounter questions you can't answer, feel free to assign it to the group as homework. Make everyone responsible to find the answer so you can discuss it next week. It doesn't have to all be on you!

Chapter Five

ENGAGING BLACK CULTS

I. The Full Picture of Black Churches

In the last chapter, we marveled at a few of the contributions of black churches. However, there are two things about black churches we must keep in mind to ensure we have a full picture:

1. **Black churches aren't perfect.** One of Dr. Eddie Glaude's strongest arguments for the death of "the Black Church" is how it has shifted from a gospel centered around Christ and His sufferings to a gospel centered around prosperity. Though the prosperity gospel is not unique to black churches and is prevalent in churches of every ethnicity, unfortunately, many public figures in black churches are agents of this false doctrine.
2. **Black churches are part of the global family of God, and are specifically tied to the history of the American Church.** Dr. Jemar Tisby, president and co-founder of The Witness, states in his Jude 3 podcast interview that "There has never not been a time when racism wasn't part of American expressions of Christianity."[52] Let that sink in for a minute. Tisby's use of the

52. Jemar Tisby, "The Truth About the American Church's Complicity in Racism" [Audio Podcast] Retrieved from https://podcasts.apple.com/us/podcast/truth-about-american-churchs-complicity-in-racism-special/id978012810?i=1000428351443 (January 2019).

word "never" is not some emotional exaggeration—it's a historical fact. In his book, *The Color of Compromise*, Tisby "takes readers on a historical journey from America's early colonial days, through slavery and the Civil War, the tragedy of Jim Crow laws, the struggles of the Civil Rights Era, up to today's Black Lives Matter Movement."[53] All along the way, the American church has unfortunately either been at the forefront of the creation and execution of these national evils, or at the forefront of standing in opposition to movements promoting civil rights.

As much as we might want to divorce ourselves from these two realities, we are wedded to them both through their leaders' and followers' professions of faith in Jesus Christ. Now we can debate all day the legitimacy of their salvation, but that's way over our pay grades. There is only one Judge, and He will judge the guilty with all righteousness and truth (Psalms 96:13). We, on the other hand, have been tasked with calling those who are far from God to plunge their sins beneath the flood of blood that was drawn from Immanuel's veins. But this task is difficult given the church's historical baggage.

Before we can even get to a conversation about the gospel, we may first be required to answer questions like, "If God is so good, why did He allow black people to suffer so horrendously?," or "If God is so powerful and just, why didn't He intervene and punish our oppressors for their sins?" Scholars refer to these seemingly "hard to answer questions" as the Problem of Evil. "The problem of evil is the question of how to reconcile the existence of evil with an omnipotent, omnibenevolent, and omniscient God."[54] The question goes, "If God is all-powerful, all-loving, and all-knowing, why do bad things happen?"

During our HBCU Tour, Lisa Fields, the founder and president of the Jude 3 Project, encountered two Hebrew Israelites at Southern University, who had come with the intention of challenging her views in a public setting. After passionately presenting their opposing view, one of the men yelled out with tears in his eyes, "Why are black people suffering like this?!" This man's cry echoes the cries of the psalmist in Psalm 22, who also felt abandoned by God. He writes,

> My God, my God, why have you abandoned me?
> Why are you so far away when I groan for help?

53. Jemar Tisby, Color of Compromise (Grand Rapids, MI: Zondervan, 2019), bill.

54. The Problem of Evil, Retrieved July 5, 2019 from https://en.wikipedia.org/wiki/Problem_of_evil

> Every day I call to you, my God, but you do not answer.
> Every night I lift my voice, but I find no relief.

Though on the surface Hebrew Israelites can appear to be just obnoxiously and aggressively shouting out obscene comments from street corners, underneath all of that vibrato is a deep sense of pain, confusion, and abandonment they long explain.

Brothers and sisters, we cannot assume that if we walk up to someone and offer them God's plan of salvation that they will just readily say, "yes!" Instead, we need to be prepared to empathize with their pain and engage their hard questions. We need to be ready to provide an apology—a reasonable argument—for how we have come to accept a religious belief that has historically been used as a tool of oppression.

How do you think someone wrestling with the problem of evil might respond to the prosperity gospel?

How would you respond to the Hebrew Israelites question, "Why are black people suffering like this?"

In general, how do you respond to friends and loved ones when they say they have turned away from the church because of its false doctrines and evil history?

II. Addressing the Problem of Evil

It's unfortunate that the message meant to give us hope in the midst of suffering has brought about sense of hopelessness for some because of its misuse. Instead of solving the problem of evil, because of its connection with the works of slavery and the institutionalization of racism, it has added more fuel to the fire and caused people to question the very character and existence of God. However, these questions are the result of a failure to get acquainted with Christianity beyond its American roots, remember that this is the same message faith that empowered the Civil Rights Movement, and carefully reflect on the gospel.

For many of us, when we think of the gospel, we only consider the cross. This makes sense given that the gospel Paul sought to pass on to the church at Corinth was that Christ had died, was buried, and had risen from the dead according to the Scriptures (1 Corinthians 15:3). However, we must remember that the cross fits within the context of a story in which God created a perfect world, then, that perfect world sinned against Him and thus became imperfect, and that through Christ's first and second coming God is and will make His world perfect again for all who confess Christ as Lord. Bad things don't happen because something is awry with God. He created the world and it was very good. Bad things happen because something is awry with humanity. When Adam and Eve sinned against God, self-centeredness, self-preservation, corruption, and every kind of wickedness along with death entered the world. God is not the one to fault or question for the brokenness of this world. Instead, we need to live in awareness of that this world is pervasively broken because of sin. The Bible says not one of us are righteous and that all of us have turn away from God (Romans 3:10). It also refers to us as inventors of evil whose feet are swift to shed blood (Romans 1:30, 3:15). So yes, we cry out with the Hebrew Israelite about the sufferings of black folks in America. It's appropriate. However, this is the bad news that has prepared our hearts to receive the Good News of Jesus Christ!

The Good News of Jesus Christ is that the all-powerful, all-loving, all-knowing, and forever wise God intervened on the behalf of humanity to rescue them from their sin and its effects by sending His one and only son, Jesus Christ, into the world to not only die for our sins, but to also sympathize with our suffering in every way (John 3:16, Hebrews 4:15). For all who trust in Him, though they will still experience trouble in this life, they can trust that in all things God is working for the good of those who love him and are called according to His purpose as they await for Christ to return and establish His kingdom (Romans 3:23-26, 8:28-30). In this new kingdom, there will be no more suffering, no more tears, no more injustice, no more grief over the pain and injustice many have experienced in this broken world (Revelation 21:4). Our all-powerful, all-loving, all-knowing, and forever wise God will wipe it all away and we will dwell in His presence day after day after day after day...

> *Group Activity:* Spend some time in prayer together by: (1) Lamenting before the Lord about past and present injustices that have taken in place in America; (2) Asking God that He would draw the hearts of those who have come to distrust Him and Christianity because of these past and present injustices to Himself.

III. Black Cults

At the 2019 Legacy Conference, as a part of the Jude 3 Apologetic's Track, Pastor Cam Triggs lead a seminar called "Black Suffering and the Problem of Evil." In addition to pointing out how many people have turned away from Christianity because of black suffering, and how it causes people to questions related to the problem, Triggs helped the audience see that many have turned to black cults because it offers them: (1) ***An identity*** that is either outside of the narrative of slavery and/or one that is superior to their white counterparts; (2) ***A destiny*** in which they are liberated from their suffering and their oppressors undergo the judgement they believe they are due.

Now, when we say "black cults," we're not talking about the charismatic movement of Jim Jones in which he convinced more than 900 people to commit suicide via a concoction of Kool-Aid, cyanide, and other deadly substances. We're talking about a group of individuals who have constructed a set of beliefs that deviate from a major religion's orthodox beliefs. For example, the Nation of Islam deviates from orthodox Islam, while the teachings of Hebrew Israelites deviate from orthodox Judaism.

Below, you will find a chart that gives a brief overview of some of the deviations and ideologies African-Americans have come to embrace in order to establish a greater sense of their identity and destiny.

Origins

The Nation of Islam was founded in 1930 by Wallace D. Fard, whom NOI followers refer to as "the Master" and believed to be the second coming of Jesus Christ. "His mission was to teach the downtrodden and defenseless Black people a thorough Knowledge of God and of themselves, and to put them on the road to Self-Independence with a superior culture and higher civilization than they had previously experienced."[55]
The honorable Elijah Muhammed was his successor and led the movement from 1934–1975. It is a sect within the Muslim faith.

Common Reasons for Rejecting Christianity

American Christianity's association with slavery, racism, and structures of oppression. They believe Christianity is like a whip in a white man's hand to keep the black man in check because of passages like, "slaves obey your masters" or "submit to governing authorities" because they have been placed there by God (Col. 3:22; Rom. 13:1–2).

Sacred and/or Important Text

They believe in the Quran and the truth of the Bible but believe "it has been tampered with and must be reinterpreted so that mankind will not be snared by the falsehoods that have been added to it."[56] When they say they believe in the truth of the Bible, they are not saying they believe the Bible is factually true. Instead, they are saying they believe the Bible has truth, in a general sense, to offer.

Elijah Muhammad's book, *A Message to the Blackman in America*, can be likened to a systematic theology book that lays out the primary beliefs of the Nation of Islam on God, humanity, salvation, the afterlife, and justice.

Doctrine of God

1. They believe that God, who they refer to as Allah, is a black man. They believe Fard was Allah in physical form.[57]

2. They deny the deity of Christ and the triune nature of God as Father, Son, and Spirit. They believe that Jesus was historically a Muslim and not Jewish.

---

55. Tynetta Muhammad, Brief History of the Origin of the Nation of Islam, Retrieved July 5th, 2019 from https://www.noi.org/noi-history/

56. Elijah Muhammad, Message to the Blackman in America (Irving, TX: Secretarius MEMPS Publication, 1965 and 1975) 163.

57. Ibid, 5.

Doctrine of Humanity

1. They believe black people are superior to all other ethnicities, particularly the white race, because the black man was the original man and all other races were created from him.[58]

2. They believe the white man is the devil.[59]

3. They believe in justice and equality for all humans regardless of their ethnicity.[60]

Doctrine of Salvation (Soteriology)

They believe black people are the fulfillment of God's promise to deliver Abraham's people from slavery.[61]

They believe black people are "the people of God's choice, as it has been written, that God would choose the rejected and the despised," and that they will receive the resurrection of the righteous because of their ethnicity and their suffering.[62]

Doctrine of the After Life

They believe in the mental—not the physical—resurrection of the dead, and believe that because they are the most in need of a mental resurrection, black people will be resurrected first.

They believe that Jesus was a Muslim and not a Jew, and that in the final judgement the white race and Christianity will be destroyed.[63]

Doctrine of Justice

They believe in justice and equality for all humans regardless of their ethnicity.[64]

---

58. Ibid, 52.

59. Ibid, 241.

60. What Muslims Want, Retrieved July 5, 2019 from https://www.noi.org/muslim-program/

61. Tynetta Muhammad, Brief History of the Origin of the Nation of Islam, Retrieved July 5th, 2019 from https://www.noi.org/noi-history/

62. Ibid.

63. Muhammad, 22.

64. What Muslims Want, Retrieved July 5, 2019 from https://www.noi.org/muslim-program/

Origins

The Hebrew Israelites trace their origins back to the Pre-Civil War Era. Their primary leaders were Frank Cherry and William Saunders Crowdy, who both believed they were commissioned as prophets by God to reveal to black people that they were the true descendants of the Hebrews spoke of in the Bible.[65] There are currently a variety of different branches of Hebrew Israelites across the country.

Common Reasons for Rejecting Christianity

Some have likened today's rise of Hebrew Israelites to that of the Nation of Islam during the Civil Rights movement, given that both of these groups are passionate about addressing the horrors of racism in America.[66] However, Hebrew Israelites don't outright reject Christianity. Instead, they have reshaped the narrative of Scripture in a way that lifts up their blackness and suffering as "*the way*" to God and excludes those who are not black or who haven't shared in the suffering of black folks from accessing eternal life.

Sacred and/or Important Text

Many believe that the King James Version of the Bible is the only authentic version, while also affirming the Apocrypha.

Doctrine of God

1. They believe God's true name is *Yah*, and that in order to be saved a person must call on the true name of Jesus in Hebrew, which is *Yahshuah Ben Yah*.

2. Many adherents reject the triune nature of God, that God is the only Supreme Being, and that Jesus was just a man.[67]

---

65. J. David Bleich, Black Jews: A Halakhic Perspective, Retrieved July 12, 2019 from http://www.jstor.org/stable/23258489

66. Jamal Hopkins, "Hebrew Israelites, KJV, & Black Identity" [Audio Podcast] Retrieved from https://podcasts.apple.com/us/podcast/jude-3-project/id978012810?i=1000430326874 (January 2019)

67. Joe Carter, 9 Things You Should Know About Black Hebrew Israelites, Retrieved July 12, 2019 from https://www.thegospelcoalition.org/article/9-things-you-should-know-about-black-hebrew-israelites/

Doctrine of Humanity
They believe "Black people are the true Israelites from the tribe of Judah" and this truth was lost as a result of the Trans-Atlantic slave trade.[68]

Doctrine of Salvation (Soteriology)
"The Black Hebrew Israelites typically believe that the Trans-Atlantic slave trade is a biblical prophecy fulfilled in our American context."[69]

Doctrine of the After Life
Many do not believe in a literal hell, but instead view the present as the white man's heaven and the black man's hell. When Jesus returns, he will gather all of Israel (black people) back to the Promised Land.[70]

68. Ryan Turner, Black Hebrew Israelites, Retrieved July 20, 2019 from https://carm.org/black-hebrew-israelites#footnote4_z4rqeh3

69. Cam Triggs, 10 Things to Study Before Engaging Hebrew Israelites, Retrieved July 15, 2019 from http://www.jude3project.com/blog/10thingstostudybhi

70. Ryan Turner, Black Hebrew Israelites, Retrieved July 20, 2019 from https://carm.org/black-hebrew-israelites#footnote4_z4rqeh3

Kemeticism

Origins

Kemeticism was revived in the late 1980s by Rev. Tamara L. Siuda, who kemets refer to as Hemet (an ancient Egyptian word translated either as "majesty" or "sacred incarnation"). It's important to note, due to its peculiarity, that Rev. Siuda is a white woman. The kemets believe she was hand-picked by the Netjer (their supreme diety) to "revive Kemet's long-forgotten ways . . . to a modern world sorely in need of it."[71]

Common Reasons for Rejecting Christianity

Believe that Christianity is an appropriation of Egyptian religions, and that it has stolen the religious legacy of people of African descent. This idea of appropriation is ever so appealing to people of African descent, given the plethora of modern examples in which white people have used certain elements of black culture for profit (i.e., Hip Hop, corn-rows, big hips and lips).

Sacred and/or Important Text

There is no sacred text associated with Kemeticism. Instead they believe in a "fluid understanding of balance, truth, and justice."

Doctrine of God

Kemeticism is polytheistic, which means they believe in many gods and goddesses. However, they do believe these deities can work together as one divine source, whom they refer to as Netjer.[72]

---

71. Rev. Tamara Siuda, Retrieved July 20, 2019 from http://www.kemet.org/nisut-biography

72. What is Kemetic Othrodoxy?, Retrieved July 20, 2019 from http://www.kemet.org/about

Pan-Africanism

Origins

The ideals of Pan-Africanism were formed in the 1850s and grew into a social and political movement that sought to reconnect African-Americans with their African roots. Though these ideals were constructed by several individuals, W. E. B. DuBois has been named the father of Pan-Africanism.[73] Today, Dr. Umar Johnson is one of the main figures of Pan-Africanism, and is affectionately referred to as "Popa"—"the prince of Pan-Africanism."[74]

Common Reasons for Rejecting Christianity

Pan-Africanism isn't so much of a rejection of Christianity, but a celebration of everything black! It is possible for a person to be both a Christian and someone who hold to ideals of Pan-Africanism. The danger is when these ideals are presented either apart from or in elevation over a biblical worldview. Several people are drawn to this ideology because it deeply affirms their blackness in a world that rarely does. If anything they would reject Christianity because historically it has demeaned, devalued, abused, and misinterpreted blackness.

Where do you see the themes of identity and destiny throughout these religions and ideologies?

What kind of identity and destiny is offered to us in the gospel?

---

73. Peter Kuryla, Pan-Africanism, Retrieved July 15, 2019 from https://www.britannica.com/topic/Pan-Africanism

74. Jerome Gay, "The Theology of Umar Johnson" [Audio Podcast] Retrieved from https://www.podbean.com/ew/pb-fr752-64a238 (November 2016).

Where are some places that you find common ground with these religions and ideologies?

What about these religions and ideologies do you find disturbing?

There is so much more that can be said and explored about each of these rising streams of thought. And because we live in an age of relativism, many who adhere to one of these ideologies may express their beliefs and practices differently from others professing the same ideals. Some will even take a little from one ideology and a little from another to create their own "unique" line of thought. Scholars refer to this practice as syncretism. So don't be surprised if you run into a person who claims to "just be spiritual and not religious" but believes black people are the original people of God and the white man is the devil, prays five times a day, attends a Christian church, and prays to his or her ancestors for wisdom. Also, be careful not to judge a person like this too quickly without getting a fuller picture of what they believe and why they believe it.

III. Principles for Engaging Black Cults

1. BE SLOW TO SPEAK AND QUICK TO LISTEN

It is very easy for us as Christians to position ourselves as those who have all the answers. It's also easy for us to get easily offended when someone says something negative or heretical about our faith. Listen, we understand the urge to want to put tape over the mouths of the men standing on street corners with bowties or cultic paraphernalia and the impulse to beat their heads over and over again with a Bible. But brothers and sisters, this is not the way. We need to be slow to speak and quick to listen (James 1:19) in hopes of getting an understanding of what they believe and why they believe it. As we slow down and listen, we get a sense of their worldview. A worldview is a set of beliefs that helps a person to make sense of the world and serves as a guide for how they will live in it. Once we have a better sense of their worldview, then we can speak directly to the concerns and beliefs they hold dear.

2. ASK GOOD QUESTIONS

Asking good questions is an important part of being slow to speak and quick to listen. Asking good questions not only gives you an opportunity to learn more about the person's worldview, but also helps you guide the conversation and keep it on track in case they go off on a tangent. Here are examples of good questions you can ask:

How did you come to accept the beliefs of ___________________?

What do you find appealing about ____________________?

How have you come to know that what you believe is true?

Anytime you sense a contradiction exist within their line of thought, question it by asking: "Earlier you said, '_____________,' but just now you said, '_______________'. How do you hold these two things in tension one another?"

What are some other good questions?

3. FIND COMMON GROUND

You may have noticed that some of what burdens and concerns those affiliated with black cults isn't far from things that burden and concern Christians. We share their disgust for the ways Christianity and the Bible was used to justify the enslavement of black people. We, too, believe in justice and equality for all. We affirm that black is beautiful, because it was created in the image of God. These are places where we can find common ground. It is in these places of common ground that we can affirm their concerns, then share how we make sense of it and respond to it through the lens of a Christian worldview.

4. KNOW WHAT YOU BELIEVE

In his podcast interview, "KJV, Hebrew Israelites, and Black Identity," Dr. Jamal

Hopkins points out that in order for a Christian to dispel the myths and misunderstandings of black cults, he or she must understand "what they believe and why they believe it."[75] This will require them to not just read the Word daily, but to study the Word in its ancient Middle-Eastern historical and cultural context. This becomes particularly significant when we are engaging with Hebrew Israelites, who use the Bible to promote and defend the majority of their claims.

Brothers and sisters, the work of knowing what you believe and why you believe it is part of your role as an ambassador for Christ (2 Corinthians 5:20). An ambassador not only accepts the decree of his or her king, but they are also intimately acquainted with King and His commands so they can intelligently share His decrees with others. Yes, this is hard work. But how else are we to plead on Christ's behalf with those caught up in false doctrines to be reconciled to God—the God who fearfully and wonderfully made them in his image; the God who never intended for them to experience the injustice of racism but created them to live in a world that was filled with perfect harmony and peace?

On the next page is a chart with a brief history of Christianity along with an overview of its primary beliefs:

75. Jamal Hopkins, "Hebrew Israelites, KJV, & Black Identity" [Audio Podcast] Retrieved from https://podcasts.apple.com/us/podcast/jude-3-project/id978012810?i=1000430326874 (January 2019.

Christianity

Origins

Christianity, which was originally referred to as "The Way," was founded by Jesus Christ between 1–4 B.C (Acts 9:2, 19:9). Jesus was a descendent of David according to the flesh, and was proclaimed to be the Son of God through His resurrection from the dead (Rom. 1:1–3). It can even be argued that Christianity started centuries prior to Jesus' resurrection given that Jesus was the fulfillment of God's promise to Adam and Eve that they would have a descendent, who would crush the head of their enemy, death and God's promise to Abraham to bless all the nations through his descendants.

Primary Beliefs

1. We believe in God the Father, who is the creator of heaven and earth and Lord over all creation.

2. We believe God the Son, Jesus Christ, born of the Virgin Mary, was both fully human and divine. We believe in His substitutionary death for all of those who would put their trust in His sacrifice on the cross for their salvation. We believe in His bodily resurrection and expect Him to return to execute justice.

3. We believe that Jesus is the only way to God based on His profession that He alone is the way, the truth, and the life, and that no one will come to the Father except through Him.

4. We believe in God the Holy Spirit, who was present at creation, participated in the resurrection, and now lives in God's people, enabling them to live the Christian life and proclaim the good news to those far from Him.

5. We believe that the Old and New Testaments together are the inspired Word of God, that it is infallible in matter of life and practice, and inerrant in its original form.

6. We believe Jesus died for the sins of the whole world, not a particular ethnic group.

7. We believe in a heaven and hell, and that those who put their faith in Jesus Christ prior to their death or His second coming will experience eternal life with Christ in heaven forever, while those who don't will spend eternity in hell apart from God.

8. We believe God has commissioned every believer to be an ambassador for Him and has empowered each of them to proclaim the gospel of Jesus Christ to the uttermost parts of the world.

5. KNOW WHY YOU BELIEVE IT

After you have plainly stated what you believe to someone who has a different worldview than you, be prepared to give a reason for why you believe it. Many Christians skip this part and simply respond to questions concerning why they believe what they believe with "I believe it because the Bible tells me so." This is no better than when you asked your parents why you can't chew gum in church and they simply responded, "Because I said so." It's not a satisfying answer. We have to remember that in most cases people have been constructing their beliefs in whatever religion they subscribe to over a period of time. You can't except to just swoop in and convince them that Jesus is the only way. You've got to be prepared to give a reasonable defense for why you hold to your beliefs. Here are a few questions you need to be prepare answer:

- Why do you believe that the Bible is true?
- Why do you believe that Jesus rose from the dead?
- Why do you believe that Jesus is not merely a man, but both human and divine?
- Why don't you believe that black people are the chosen people of God?
- Why don't you believe that the white man is the devil?
- Why do you believe that salvation is for everyone who believes in Jesus Christ?
- Why do you think that Christianity and the Bible affirm blackness?

Group Activity: If you are in a group, practice with each other how you might answer some of these questions. At the end of each person's turn, give one another feedback on what the person did well and where they can improve. Hold each other accountable to doing the hard work of learning how to provide answers to each of these questions.

6. CONTEND FOR THE FAITH

One of the Hebrew Israelites' foundational passages of Scripture is Deuteronomy 28. When they read Deuteronomy 28 they find an answer to the Hebrew Israelites question, "Why are black people suffering like this?"

On a Hebrew Israelite website, dueteronomony28.org, at the top of their home page it reads, "YAH (God) said that He would curse Israel for their disobedience and those curses would be used as a sign to identify who the true children of Israel are!"

As a group read Deuteronomy 28 and discuss the following questions:

In what ways are the Hebrew Israelites drawing parallels between the curses presented in Deuteronomy 28 and black suffering?

What do you find problematic about their interpretation of this passage of Scripture?

In the first chapter of this book, we answered the question, "What is Hermeneutics?" What we decided to hold off telling you about until this very opportune time is that there are two common hermeneutical processes: exegesis and eisegesis. Exegesis is the process by which the reader studies a passage of scripture with the intention of drawing out the author's intended meaning in light of the author's historical and cultural context. Eisegesis, on the other hand, is the process by which the reader imposes their interpretation and 21st century context onto the text. For example, many people claim the promise God made to the children of Israel in Jeremiah 29:11 for themselves. Now, I'm not saying that the Lord doesn't have a plan for your life or that He doesn't want you to prosper, but that promise was not made to you. That's eisegesis. That promise was made to the people of Israel when they were defeated and taken captive by the Babylonians. Imagine their confusion. Here they are the very people of God and they have been removed from the very land that God promised them. Then God tells them that He is actually the one who has brought this judgment on them in order for them to repeat. And though they might understand that there are consequences for their sins, they now find themselves captives to some of the biggest idolaters in the known world. It's into this confusion that God speaks these words to Israel, "I know the plans that I have for you...they are plans for good and not disaster, to give you a future and a hope" (Jeremiah 29:11).

This is the same thing that the Hebrew Israelites are doing when they say, "Since the curses in Deuteronomy are closely related to the experiences we had during slavery, it must be talking about us." However, if you keep reading through the Old Testament you will see that Israel bore the consequences of their sins when they were exiled from their homeland and taken as captives by the Babylonian Empire. Remember Daniel? Daniel was a slave as a fulfillment of these curses. All throughout the book of Lamentations the writer records his grieve over how the very things that God said would happen, happened.

> "Judah has been led away into captivity,
> oppressed with cruel slavery.
> She lives among foreign nations
> and has no place to rest" (Lamentations 1:3).
>
> "The Lord is just,
> for I have rebelled against his commands.
> Listen, all you people;
> look at my pain.
> my young women and young men
> have gone into captivity" (Lamentations 1:18).
>
> "Lord, look and consider
> To whom you have done this.
> Should women eat their own children,
> The infants they have nurtured" (Lamentations 2:20)?

Though the writer of Lamentations shares the same confusion as the Hebrew Israelites over the state of his people, he doesn't share his ethnicity. And here's the beauty of it: He doesn't have to in order to be fully assured that God sees him, loves him, and will rescue him for his sins.

> "In this the love of God was made manifest among us, that God sent his only Son into the world, so that we might live through him. In this is love, not that we have loved God but that he loved us and sent his Son to be the propitiation for our sins" (1 John 4:9-10, ESV)

That big word, "propitiation," means that Christ satisfied the wrath of God against our sins through His life, death, and resurrection. If this is true, then this means that God has no more curses to deal out because of sin. Instead, all of God's beef with humanity was squashed at the cross. We can trust that Jesus' sacrifice was sufficient for all of us because in raising from the dead, he conquered our greatest enemy, death! This is the gospel! This is our hope! Let us follow the apostle Peter's instruction and revel in the beauty of the gospel for our own soul's sake so that we will be ready to give a defense with gentleness and respect to all who would ask us to give a reason for the hope we have within (1 Peter 3:13-17).

Challenge: Sign up to the Old Testament Bible Reading Plan on our Jude 3 Project Bible Reading App as a way to get familiar with the story of God. This step alone will serve you greatly in your ability to contend for the faith against heresy.

IV. Tools for Going Deeper

- Jemar Tisby, Color of Compromise (Grand Rapids, MI: Zondervan, 2019).
- Rahaan A. Armand and Tyran T. Laws, The Round Table: A Christian's Conversation with Marginal Beliefs Affecting the Black Church Experience (USA: Xulon Press).

Leader's Guide

CHAPTER SIX

Objective

To provide participants with a hermeneutical process for interpreting difficult texts in the Bible.

Big Ideas

1. "The Bible ain't no PG book!" It is filled with war, incest, rape, injustice, slavery, murder, horror, love stories, and the story of an innocent man who was sentenced to severe flogging and death on the cross. You need to know these stories. Many people have rejected God because they can't understand why these things would be in His book.
2. Difficult passages can be understood; you just have to do the work. In this chapter, you will be presented with several principles that will help you interpret and understand some of the most difficult passages in the Bible.
3. Understand the difference between descriptive and prescriptive text. Descriptive texts are narratives that tell us a story. When telling a story, the Bible neither condones or approves a person's behavior. Prescriptive texts are prepositional statements that tell us how to live. They put before us behaviors that are either approved or condemned by God.

JUDE 3 PROJECT

Podcast Playlist

"Slavery and the Bible"
Guest: Dr. Esau McCaulley
Date: July 2017

"Is God a Sexist?"
Guest: Dr. Joanne Vitale
Date: November 2018

Helpful Tips

Tip 1: Just like last time, select the paragraphs and sections you would like to read together before working through your group's questions.

Tip 2: Go and listen to these podcasts! They are the BOMB! Both Dr. McCaulley and Dr. Vitale provide us with a helpful framework for how to interpret difficult passages in the Bible.

Tip 3: This is probably the most interactive chapter of the book. Be prepared to do less talking.

Chapter Six

PLACES OF CONTENTION

I. Places of Contention in the Bible

Have you ever been reading the Bible and had to come to a complete stop because something you read seemed deeply problematic? Maybe you read something horrific that caused you to question the goodness of God. Maybe something just rubbed you the wrong way.

If this has happened to you, good. As our sister Ekemini Uwan said at the 2019 Courageous Conversation conference, "The Bible ain't no PG book."[76] It is filled with war, incest, rape, injustice, slavery, murder, horror, love stories, and the story of an innocent man who was sentenced to severe flogging and death on the cross.

If the Bible hasn't made you uncomfortable yet, just keep reading it. Abandon your tendency to hop around the Bible from one favorite passage to the next and read it from Genesis 1:1 to Revelation 22:19. Resist the temptation to skip over the books that seem irrelevant to you. Those seemingly irrelevant books usually find themselves at the forefront of theological debate. Remember Deuteronomy 28? Hebrew Israelites have built a whole religion around that one chapter of the Bible. Don't allow fear

76. Dr. Charlie Dates, Willie Francios, Dr. Nichielle Guirdy, and Ekimini Uwan, "Discerning Truth", Retrieved August 8, 2019 from https://www.courageousconvos.org/2019-conversations

to cause you to ignore those passages in the Bible that seem to stand in contention with what you have come to understand about God or Christianity. Instead, sit there, wrestle with your complex questions, and pray. Our Father will gladly meet you there.

In this chapter, we are going to deal with some seemingly contentious places in the Bible. We will do this by first laying out some general principles for how to interpret difficult passages in the Bible. Then, we will deal with two problematic passages in the Bible—one on the treatment of women, the other on slavery.

Are there some Bible passages that seem disturbing, confusing, or contradictory to you? If so, list them here and discuss your questions with the group. Don't try to answer one another's questions right now. Just listen. Learn to be OK with living in those places of contention together.

II. Principles for Interpreting Difficult Passages in the Bible

1. GENRE MATTERS

There really isn't any other book like the Bible. It is comprised of sixty-six books, was written by forty different authors, spans about 7,000 years of history, and utilizes more than ten different genres to tell one cohesive story about God and humanity. In his book *A Layperson's Guide to Biblical Interpretation,* Dr. Luke Bobo reminds us that "while, all genres operate on our imaginations, emotions (heart), intellects, and wills—they do so differently."[77] Poetry engages our imagination and emotions in ways a narrative never could. The instruction given in wisdom literature like Proverbs and Ecclesiastes should be read and interpreted differently than the instruction Paul lays out in his epistles (letters) to churches. Here are some of the major genres in the Bible, along with a brief summary of how each one of them is utilized in the Bible to tell one cohesive story.

77. Luke Brad Bobo, A Layperson's Guide To Biblical Interpretation: A Means to Know the Personal God (Eugene, OR: Resource Publications 2016), 69.

Literary Genre	*Summary*	*Examples*
Historical Narrative	Historical Narratives "simply recount the past."[78] They make up about 60% of the Bible and function as a descriptive text that informs us of what happened in the past rather than a prescriptive text that instructs us on how to live in the present.[79]	Genesis, Judges, Daniel 1–6, Ruth, 1 Samuel, 2 Chronicles, Matthew, Luke, Acts
Law	When scholars speak of law as a genre of the Bible, they are referring to the laws recorded in Exodus, Leviticus, Numbers, and Deuteronomy. These laws were given to Israel to govern their covenantal relationship with God. Though the law may seem to lack relevance today because it was fulfilled in Christ and Christians are no longer bound to the law, it still has immense value to us. They "provide timeless ethical, moral, and theological principles," while also revealing to us "the character of God and our need for the Perfect Law Keeper, Jesus Christ."[80]	Leviticus, Numbers, Deuteronomy
Poetry	Poetry is a wonderfully complex genre of the Bible. Biblical authors used this genre to communicate their pain, talk out their confusion, express their truest loves, and awaken their audiences' hearts with rich and powerful language. Poetry humanizes the Bible by helping us understand how David felt when he was being unjustly pursued by Saul or how Israel emotionally navigated their years of exile in Babylon.	Psalm 19, Psalm 23, Hosea 2, Lamentations, John 1:1–5, and Philippians 2:6–11

78. Ibid, 82.

79. Robert L. Plummer, 40 Questions About Interpreting the Bible (Grand Rapids, MI: Kregel Publishing 2010), 191.

80. Bobo, 81.

Wisdom	Wisdom is likely one of the most misinterpreted and misapplied genres of the Bible. This is likely because many have interpreted it's causal nature of "if you do this, then this will happen" as sure promises of the Bible. However, "a proverb contains a principle, not a promise. A proverb tells you: this is how life basically works. What is left unsaid is the qualifier: life does not always, 100 percent of the time, work this way."[81]	Job, Proverbs, and Ecclesiastes
Prophecy	Though many of the prophets foretold the future, their primary role was to call the Israelites back into proper fellowship with God by *turning away* from idolatrous and injustice behaviors and *turning* to obedience of God's commands. Many of the events they foretold were even in relation to Israel's and other nations' disobedience and how God would respond if they didn't repent. Many of "these 'future events' were immediately fulfilled in the lifecycles of Israel, Judah or surrounding nations."[82]	Isaiah, Obadiah, Micah
Letters	"Of the twenty-seven books in the New Testament, twenty-one are letters. Some are letters to individuals, but most are written to congregations."[83] Reading letters can very much feel like eavesdropping on someone's phone conversation. Though we can hear what the person near us is saying, we have no idea what the person on the other end of the phone has said or done to necessitate their response. For that reason, it is very important to read, study, and interpret these letters in light of their historical and cultural contexts to ensure we don't read our twenty-first century experience into the text.	Romans, 1 Corinthians, 2 Corinthians, Galatians, Ephesians, Philippians, Colossians, 1–2 Thessalonians, 1–2 Timothy, Titus, Philemon, Hebrews, James, 1–2 Peter, 1–3 John, Jude

81. Howard G. Hendricks and William D. Hendricks, Living by the Book: The Art and Science of Reading the Bible (Chicago: IL Moody Publishers, 2007), Kindle Locations 4401-4402.

82. Bobo, 84.

83. Plummer, 279.

 ***Apocalyptic***	Apocalyptic literature is one of the strangest literary genres of the Bible due to the richness of its symbolic imagery and its ambiguous language.[84] It is best to stay away from literal interpretations of this genre and to be content with not fully grasping its meaning. Instead, pay attention to overarching themes of the text.	Daniel 7–12, Revelations

2. CONTEXT MATTERS

We will never grow tired of stating the importance of context in the task of interpreting Scripture. Though we have already mentioned a few throughout the book, here is a list of the different contexts we need to consider when interpreting Scripture, along with a brief definition:

> *Literary Context:* Every verse exists within a paragraph, that exists within a chapter, that exists within a book, that exists within a testament, that exists within the Bible. Sometimes we can find the answers to our questions if we just keep reading. For instance, if you are reading John 3:16 and find yourself wondering what the eternal life is that Jesus is talking about, just keep reading. You'll find your answer in John 17:3.

How does Jesus define eternal life in John 17:3?

How does this expand your understanding of eternal life and your relationship with God?

84. Bobo, 89.

When we pluck a verse out of its literary context, we will often walk away with either a shortsighted or completely wrong interpretation. We will also likely miss the author's intended purpose for writing those particular words. If we just did the work of regular ol' reading and comprehension, we would find that some of the passages we think are mysterious and difficult to interpret are really quite simple.

Historical Context: As stated in the chart above, reading the Bible can be a lot like eavesdropping on a phone conversation. For that reason, sometimes we need to seek out resources like commentaries and Bible dictionaries to get a better sense of what's going on historically and how it gave rise to the words we see on the pages of Scripture. For instance, consider what the disciples asked Jesus right before his ascension: "Lord, has the time come for you to free Israel and restore our kingdom?" (Acts 1:6). This may seem like a silly question to us, but when we familiarize ourselves with the historical context their question becomes clear.

Remember Jeremiah 29:11? God promised Israel that though they were in exile and under Babylonian rule, He had a plan for them to prosper and to give them a better future. Israel had always interpreted that as the redemption of their land and being freed from the rule of their enemies. About 600 years later, Israel found themselves not under the rule of another empire—Rome. Knowing that, the disciples' question is not so silly anymore, is it? They were probably thinking, "This is Jesus, the one who said He had come to set the captive free and who rose from the dead. If he resurrected Himself, surely he can overthrow a whole kingdom, right?"

Look at how Jesus responds in Acts 1:7-8 : "The Father alone has the authority to set those dates and times, and they are not for you to know. But you will receive power when the Holy Spirit comes upon you. And you will be my witnesses, telling people about me everywhere—in Jerusalem, throughout Judea, in Samaria, and to the ends of the earth."

He redirected their focus from just the redemption of land to the redemption of souls. He emphasized the eternal need for people to be freed from the captivity of the evil one rather than their desire to be freed from Roman rule. "That will come, but for now be my witnesses in all of the earth," he says.

Cultural Context: Many have likened opening the pages of Scripture to entering a foreign country in which they greet one another with a kiss or words like "shalom" instead of a hearty "what's good, fam?" It's different. Instead of sitting up straight at the dinner table, they recline, which today would be considered not having good manners. When a woman's husband dies, she is left with very little options for providing for herself. Therefore, when Jesus raises the wailing woman's son from the dead in Luke 7:11–17 he is not only demonstrating his great power, but also his compassionate heart. Jesus knows her life will be bitter without the presence of a man to protect and provide for her in her ancient Middle Eastern society. Jesus knows she can't just pull herself up by her boot straps, get a job, and become an independent woman. Though this kind of cultural reality makes us cringe and is nonsense to us in a time when women are raising families on their own with brilliance and grace, we have to be careful of what Dr. Joanne Vitale refers to as chronological snobbery.[85] We need to be careful to not judge a 3,000-year-old culture that we don't quite understand, and instead humbly wrestle with its cultural differences in an honest yet respectful way.

Redemptive Context: The story of God in the Bible moves in a particular direction. It moves from the creation of all things, to the fall of all things, to the rescue of all things, to its final redemption. We must keep this metanarrative (overarching story) of the Bible in mind when we encounter not just difficult passages, but all passages. This becomes particularly important when we are confronted with the horrors of sin and injustice in the Bible. The metanarrative of Scripture keeps us from blaming God for the wretchedness of this world and helps us remember that the world we live in is very different from the world He created. He told Adam and Eve not to eat from the tree of the knowledge of good and evil because He never wanted them to know the bitter taste of selfishness, murder, incest, betrayal, abandonment, rape, slavery, and so much more. He was so grieved by sin and its effects on humanity that He sent Christ to intervene on our behalf and rescue us from the penalty and power of sin. And, soon He will rescue all who have trusted in Christ for their salvation from sin's destruction. This is the lens we need to read the Bible through for our faith to not be deterred when we encounter tough passages like that of the Levite's concubine in Judges 19. Passages like Judge 19 exist not to challenge the goodness of God, but instead to confirm the reality of the fallen condition of the human heart.

85. Joanne Vitale, "Is God a Sexist?" [Audio Podcast], Retrieved from https://jude3project.podbean.com/?s=Is+God+Sexist November 2018

How does Judges 19 testify to the fallen condition of humanity?

In her podcast interview, Joanne Vitale expounds on this text in a way that invites us to wrestle with the question, "Why is this passage in the Bible?" Given that the Bible is the inspired Word of God, what might God be trying to reveal to us through this story?

Vitale reminds us that throughout the book of Judges everybody in Israel is said to be doing right in their own eyes. Judges 19—these acts of horror against this nameless concubine—is what happens when people turn from the goodness of God's instruction and try to define what is right for themselves.

3. CROSS-REFERENCES MATTER

Here's an important rule of thumb: When the Bible is clear on something in one passage and seems confusing in another, go with what has been made clear. In your Bible (your paper Bible, that is) you will find tiny letters dispersed throughout the verses. These letters are footnotes that direct you to other passages in the Bible that are related to the one you're reading. These other passages are referred to as cross-references. If one of those tiny letters shows up in a passage you are finding difficult to understand, reading the cross-references can be extremely helpful. For instance, remember our brief discussion of Deuteronomy 28 and Lamentations in the previous chapter? If you found that impressive, don't. It was just a little exercise of paying attention to those little letters and reading the cross-references.

> *Group Activity:* Open your Bible to the book of Lamentations. In the middle (or the bottom) of your Bible you should find a list of cross-references that correspond with the verses in Lamentations. Using the list of cross-references as a guide, note which verses in Lamentations overlap with verses in Deuteronomy 28. The first one has been done for you.

Lamentations	**Deuteronomy 28**
Lamentation 1:3	Deuteronomy 28:65

***You can find the answer key at the end of the chapter.*

How do these cross-references further discredit the claims of Hebrew Israelites?

4. COMMUNITY MATTERS

When Jesus ascended into the heavens, he left us with His Spirit, His Word, and His Spirit-filled people to comfort and lead us into all truth. This is extremely loving of God, given that our hearts—though redeemed by Christ's blood—are still deceitful and tempt us to stray away from the Lord's instruction. These three gifts keep us safe from falling into despair and heresy in our attempts to interpret difficult passages of Scripture. So don't let pride or shame keep you from raising your hand in Bible study to ask a seemingly stupid question. And don't let fear of what you will find keep you from wrestling with hard questions about life and the Bible. Seek out God's people for help. Whether it be asking your pastor or Sunday school teacher directly, picking up a book, or listening to a podcast, use all the resources God has provided.

Who are some men and women in your life that are well-acquainted with Scripture that might be able to answer your questions about the Bible?

Who are some Christian scholars and thought-leaders you can spend more time with by reading books, listening to sermons, or attending a conference?

III. The Bible and Women

Many women (and men) have read the Bible and accused "Old Testament writers of endorsing all kinds of sexism, patriarchy (socially oppressive structures favoring men over women), and even misogyny (hatred of women)."[86]

What are some passages in the Bible concerning women that seem problematic to you?

When asked a similar question, Dr. Vitale responded,

> Across the Old Testament you have rape, polygamy, incest, (and) violence against women. It's all in the text. . . . Before jumping to the conclusion that [these stories] are here because God thinks they are a good idea . . . Could it be that [these stories] are not there to commend the behavior but actually to condemn it in the strongest possible way? And could it be that the Bible is intended to be a kind of story that depicts both the highs [and] also the extreme lows of

86. Paul Copan, Is God a Moral Monster?: Making Sense of the Old Testament God (Grand Rapids:MI Bakers Books, 2011), 101.

human nature? And a lot of these extreme lows involve the way that women have been treated throughout history.

For me, the hardest [passages used to be] a lot of the narratives, but I don't find those to be the hardest. . . . What I find the hardest [now] are the legal codes . . . because when it comes to the narratives in the Old Testament you can say, "Well, these are here as examples of people behaving badly to show how messed up the world is and how much we need saving." But, what about the legal codes? If they are laws given by God, then how do you make sense of the fact that some of those laws are hard to come to grips with? If God is perfect and eternal then whenever he gives laws then those laws must also be perfect and eternal, [right]? For a long time that was the assumption I came to when reading that genre of the Bible. . . . But then, I think part of learning for me has been coming to understand what is the function of these legal codes and coming to understand that they're really intended for a particular time and a particular place in history, kind of like case laws or provisional laws.

[For example] if a teenager [wants to do] something stupid and [their] parents really don't want them to do it. So, they're like, "Hey, I don't want you to go out but at least be home by midnight," or "I don't want you to get your nose pierced, but if you're going to get it pierced at least take it out when Grandma comes to stay." It's basically like [saying] "I don't want you to do these things, but I know what you are like [and] I know you're going to do them, so let's put some things in place to manage human mess as far as possible." . . . So some of the legal codes we read [in the Old Testament] are dealing with really tricky and messy situations that God is trying to, I would say, limit the damage as much as possible.[87]

What are some of the principles listed above that Dr. Vitale is using to explain how she interacts with difficult passages about women in the Bible?

---

87. Joanne Vitale, "Is God a Sexist?" [Audio Podcast], Retrieved from https://jude3project.podbean.com/?s=Is+God+Sexist November 2018

Let's look at one of these legal codes Dr. Vitale is referring to using the principles above. Read Deuteronomy 21:10–14 and use the following questions as a guide for applying the principles for interpreting difficult passages of Scripture.

Genre

What is the genre of this passage?

Is this a descriptive or prescriptive text? If prescriptive, to whom is the command given?

Literary Context

What book of the Bible is this passage in?

What are some of the unique features of this book that you need to keep in mind to ensure you interpret this passage correctly?

Read Deuteronomy 20–22. How does the literary context help you get a better understanding of what is happening in Deuteronomy 21:10–14?

How does Deuteronomy 22:13-30 affirm the equality of man and women?

How does Deuteronomy 22:13-30 affirm God's desire to protect and care for women?

Historical Context

Where does this story fit within the historical timeline of Israel's history? Where have they been, and where are they going?

Cultural Context

What are some cultural norms in this Deuteronomy 21:10–14 that are not normative for our culture today?

In what ways do you need to be careful to not commit cultural snobbery?

What questions do you need to ask about this culture to ensure you interpret this passage well?

In what ways do you see God managing the mess of humanity?

Redemptive Context

Creation: How does the creation story keep us from falling into the belief that God views women as less than men? (Hint: see Genesis 1:27.)

Fall: In what ways does this passage reveal the wickedness of the human heart?

Rescue: In what ways do God's legal codes seek to rescue women from abuse and harm?

How does the gospel keep us from falling into the belief that God views women as less than men? (Hint: Galatians 3:27–28)

Final Redemption: Though women were and still do experience different levels of sexism and misogyny, what hope can be found for justice and freedom in the second coming of Christ?

Cross-References

Are there any cross references in this text that need to be considered?

How has applying these principles helped you to get a better understand of Deuteronomy 21:10–14?

What about this passage still makes you uncomfortable?

How might you summarize this text given what you have learned?

If someone was to say to you, "I just can't get down with the Bible. All it does is promote a misogynistic, sexist, and patriarchal culture," how would you respond? Remember to affirm their pain and concerns before offering a response.

IV. The Bible and Slavery

Well, there it is—slavery. Right there in our Bible. Both the Old and the New Testament contain passages about slavery. What are we supposed to do with these texts? Here's how Dr. Esau McCaulley responds to this question:

> I actually don't usually start off with the particular passages that deal with slavery. I actually try to give them a hermeneutic, or way of looking at the Bible as a whole. . . . Interestingly enough, I actually like to start with what Jesus said about divorce. That may seem like a strange place to start off talking about slavery, but I think it gives us a hermeneutical key to understanding how we read the Bible, especially the Old Testament laws. In that passage . . . the Pharisees and the Sadducees . . . come to Jesus and they asked him, "Jesus, Moses said that we can divorce our wife for any reason. What do you think?"
>
> What they really wanted to do is similar to what we do in the slavery issue, they want to get Jesus into the weeds to fight about all of these different passages to catch him in this exegetical conundrum. What Jesus does is he goes, "Well, hold on in the beginning, it wasn't that way." So rather than actually beginning with the passages in Deuteronomy, he actually goes back to creation and say what was God's creational intent? He says God's creational intent was for man and woman to be united as one flesh. Every

law that Moses has about divorce, was actually because of Israel's hardness of heart. So in other words he's saying . . . God put these certain laws [in place] to deal with human sinfulness. . .

So I think . . . we take a step back, look at the Bible as a whole [and ask ourselves], do we have any evidence that it was God's creational intent to enslave people? . . . When we read the Genesis creation story, does it seem like God's plan was we're going to have slaves? . . . Well, of course not. So that means that what slavery then is, or at least the discussion of the Bible . . . are God's attempts to mitigate the impact of human sin. . . . So the statement that the Bible support slavery to me just misunderstands how Christians read the Bible. Just because there's a passage that talks about something, it doesn't mean that that's commended as the way that God expects a society to function.[88]

Which of the principles listed above is Dr. McCaulley using to explain how he interacts with difficult passages about slavery in the Bible?

Let's look at Colossians 3:22 using our principles for interpretation. Use the following questions as a guide for applying the principles for interpreting difficult passages of Scripture.

88. Esau McCaulley, "Slavery and the Bible" [Audio podcast], Retrieved from https://www.podbean.com/ew/pb-pprxw-6d1928 July 2017

Lamentations	Deuteronomy 28
Lamentation 1:3	Deuteronomy 28:65
Lamentations 1:5	Deuteronomy 28:13
Lamentations 1:9	Deuteronomy 28:43
Lamentations 1:14	Deuteronomy 28:48
Lamentations 1:18	Deuteronomy 28:41
Lamentations 2:12	Deuteronomy 28:51
Lamentations 2:16	Deuteronomy 28:37
Lamentations 2:20	Deuteronomy 28:53–57
Lamentations 4:10	Deuteronomy 28:53
Lamentations 4:14	Deuteronomy 28:29

Genre	What is the genre of this passage? Is this a descriptive or prescriptive text? If prescriptive, to whom is the command given?
Literary Context	What book of the Bible is this passage in? What are some of the unique features of this book that you need to keep in mind to ensure you interpret this passage correctly? Read Colossians 3:1–4:1. How does the literary context help you get a better understanding of what is happening in Colossians 3:22? How might a Christian who is a slave and worships at the church at Colossae find comfort in Colossians 3:25? How might a Christian who owns slaves and worships at the church at Colossae be convicted by Colossians 3:25–4:1?
Historical Context	Where does this story fit within the historical timeline of the history of the church? Keep in mind that Christianity was new at the time, and many Gentiles who had lived apart from God and his commands had little to no idea of how to live in a way that honors the Lord. Is it fair to assume that every Christian slave had a Christian slave owner?
Cultural Context	What are some cultural norms in the church at Colossae that are not normative for our culture today? In what ways do you need to be careful to not commit cultural snobbery? What questions do you need to ask about this culture to ensure you interpret this passage well?

Redemptive Context

Creation: How does the creation story keep us from falling into the belief that God affirms slavery?

Fall: In what ways does this passage reveal the wickedness of the human heart?

Rescue: How does the gospel keep us from falling into the belief that God views women as less than men? (Hint: see Galatians 3:27–28.)

Final Redemption: What hope and comfort did Colossians 3:22–4:1 offer to those living in slavery?

Cross References

Are there any cross references in this text that need to be considered? (Hint: Passages in Ephesians, 1 Corinthians about slavery.)

Read Exodus 21. In what ways do you see God managing the mess of humanity?

How is slavery within this cultural context different than American slavery?

How has applying these principles helped you to get a better understanding of Colossians 3:22?

What about this passage still makes you uncomfortable?

How might you summarize this text given what you have learned?

If someone was to say to you, "I just can't get down with the Bible because it affirms slavery and white men used it to enslave our people," how would you respond? Remember to affirm their pain and concerns before offering a response.

V. Why do these passages bother us?

Why do these passages bother us so much? Why do they cause us to question the goodness of God? The nagging feelings of anger, sadness, and confusion we encounter when we read this kind of text reminds us that we we're not created to live in this kind of world. This is also true for the feminist that feels ostracized and person of color who feels ignored and oppressed when they open the pages of Scripture. We're all groaning with pains for the new heaven and the new earth. We all want out of this sinful and broken world. Our pains testify to our beliefs that God is good.

But what if these stories are in the Bible to help us to see that our good God doesn't look away from the evilness of this world? That instead of looking away, He stares at it with us and is grieved by it even more than us? Not only does he look at it, but He comes down in the form of Christ to do something about it! He intervenes! He inserts Himself into humanity's mess. He takes on all our sins and our pains. And in His resurrection, He liberates us from sin's power! Soon, He will liberate us from its presence!

Yes, this has already been said, but the gospel is the lens through we are to interpret these kinds of passages in the Bible. It is also the lens through which we are to interpret the most horrific moments of our lives. The same principles we use to interpret difficult passages in the Bible can be used to interpret the hardships you experience in this life. We need these passages. Without them we fall into a false sense of reality that the Christian life is void of pain and struggle. But God's people struggled and often lived under oppression. Women navigated faulty cultural norms. Slaves endured under the harshness of men and women they also worshipped with on Sunday mornings.

Though we are far removed from this historical time period, we still feel its effects. However, we can be assured that God sees, God knows, and He will act.

VI. Tools for Going Deeper

- Bobo, Luke Brad. A Layperson's Guide to Biblical Interpretation: A Means to Know the Personal God. Eugene, Oregon: Resource Publications, 2016.
- Copan, Paul. Is God a Moral Monster?. Grand Rapids, MI: Baker Books, 2011.
- Plummer, Robert L. 40 Questions About Interpreting the Bible. Grand Rapids, MI: Kregel Publications, 2006.

Made in the USA
Monee, IL
16 July 2022

99850250R00066